For the Boss

7.30 AM. forecast 32 lovely clear
morning heavy dew — early morn
spent with Hubert cleaning
diseased leaves from under
Rhododendrons — remainder
of morning employed in N.E.
dead heading — garden
holding well — white easter daisy
a dream — productive
afternoon spent with Dawn
in pool area. — trim steps
cut out over fronds of
ferns — shaped Toronas cut
off seed pods + fed with
blood + bone / plants have
lost their colour — most
pleasant 30 mins shared our
Pritors catalogue + afternoon
tea pot. — choosing roses
to be ordered this
season — . Also discussed
having a timber structure

in the picking garden to grow
a climbing Titan — in
order to carry the roses on
from the four bed beds to
the climbing Peace at the
glass house — also pick up
Titan Hedge — thus giving
a better overall feel of Roses
to the over all size of the
garden.

Top Temp 30

While working in pool area
self & D.C. drew suggestions
into the pot re the placing
of the column in the garden
D.C. suggested Dove cote or
figure — mine garden lamp
beyond stables, both agreed
column must be in sight of
side porch or front columns.

Cruden Farm

Garden Diaries

——— ❧ ———

M ICHAEL M ORRISON

& L ISA C LAUSEN

Photography by Simon Griffiths

LANTERN

an imprint of
PENGUIN BOOKS

Front drive

Round lawn

Pool

Walled Garden

Tool room

Stables' dam

Picking Garden

Stables

Nursery

Compost

Back drive

Post-and-rail fence

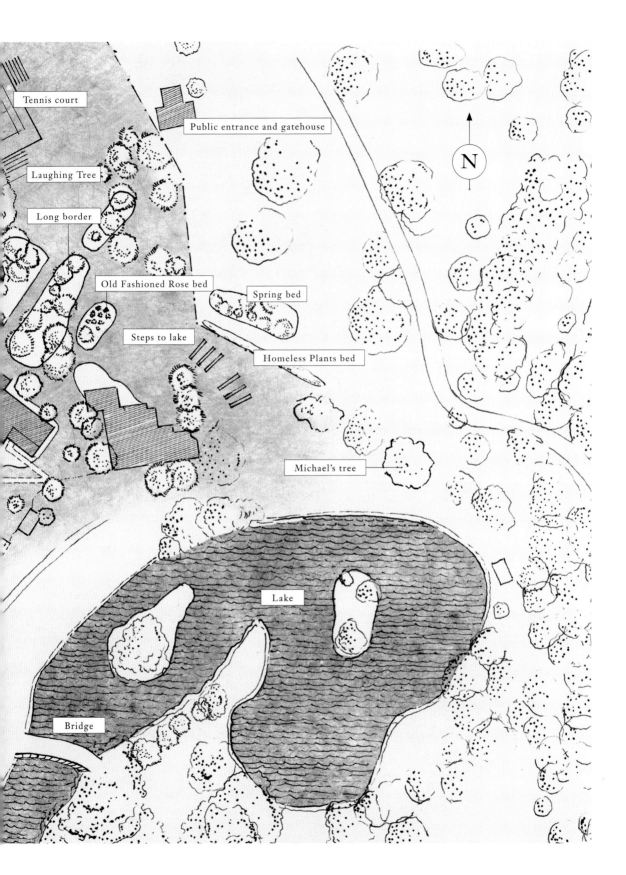

Tennis court

Public entrance and gatehouse

Laughing Tree

Long border

Old Fashioned Rose bed

Spring bed

Steps to lake

Homeless Plants bed

Michael's tree

N

Lake

Bridge

Foreword

Cruden Farm was the home of my much loved grandmother, the late Dame Elisabeth Murdoch, for eighty years. The beautiful garden at Cruden Farm was a great passion of hers and, although Granny always said she had not created a garden but had landscaped a farm, the garden is now admired throughout Australia and treasured by many thousands of visitors each year.

In 1971 Granny was fortunate to find a kindred spirit in gardener Michael Morrison, who came to share her passion for Cruden Farm. They worked together with great creativity, dedication and pleasure for 41 years. We are delighted that Michael agreed to share his personal story and garden diaries in this book.

Granny always maintained that Michael was like a second son to her and as a team they were formidable. Michael always credited 'the Boss' with making every decision regarding the garden but after so many years of working side by side we think it is obvious they created much of Cruden Farm together. They spent hours talking, planning, touring and making sure every decision about the garden and farm was well thought through.

These decisions and daily events in the garden were all noted in Michael's diaries and it's very special to have this archive. The diaries are a wonderful memento of Granny, and reflect much of her character and spirit, but importantly they also form a superb historical record that allows the garden to be maintained with her vision and foresight.

Cruden's oldest trees, such as the *Quercus* 'Firthii' planted as a seedling by Dame Elisabeth, define the garden she and Michael created.

Lisa Clausen has managed to capture the magic of Cruden Farm with her beautifully written words that incorporate the history of the garden, intertwined with extracts from Michael's diaries. Having watched them work together, it is apparent that they have formed a close bond and we are very grateful to Lisa for her time, passion and commitment to the project.

Michael Morrison is a special person. We recognise that it is rare for one individual to be so dedicated to the place we all love and we are so grateful to Michael for his loyalty. Granny and Michael shared a common outlook on life – the importance of always looking to the future while still honouring the past. We are all comforted that Michael, with all his wisdom and knowledge, remains at Cruden Farm as the garden continues to grow and have an ongoing life.

On behalf of our family, we look forward to Cruden Farm's future and we hope to ensure it remains a place of beauty that can be shared by all – a garden that is both viable and sustainable for future generations to enjoy.

~ Penny Fowler

Delphinium in the informal and colour-filled flower beds that are central to Cruden's enduring beauty.

OPPOSITE Michael weeding the Front Border, one of the many beds he's cared for since 1971.

CHAPTER ONE

A Stroke of Luck

D awn is near and Cruden Farm is waking beneath a canvas of purple and blue, shot through with ribbons of gold. As birds begin filling the garden with song, soft light drifts among the flowers and trees, before suddenly illuminating the dark lake with rose-streaked reflections of the breaking dawn. The white-haired gardener watching quietly from the water's edge never tires of this spectacle, though he has seen it many times. He's no longer the young man who first explored this garden almost half a century ago, and hobbles now as he walks, a favourite pair of secateurs in his pocket. But Michael Morrison's love for Cruden has only grown through the years, and is now as certain as daybreak itself.

> Another wonderful morning. So difficult to get on – just want to go on walking & soaking all this beauty in. *~ JANUARY 31, 1993*

It was a Sunday afternoon in the spring of 1971 when Michael pulled up in his ute at the white-columned porch of Elisabeth Murdoch's home to talk about a gardening job. She was then sixty-two, a well-travelled and tireless philanthropist, matriarch of a wealthy and successful family and the widow of newspaper proprietor Sir Keith Murdoch. Her life was very different from that of the quiet twenty-seven-year-old landscaper from country Victoria who had never been overseas. It was a meeting which owed much to luck. The Dame happened to ask friends if they could recommend a gardener; Michael was thinking of starting up his own

Early morning's glow in the Picking Garden.

landscaping business. Fortunately for Cruden, he arranged to visit the Dame instead.

She poured Michael a cup of tea in her elegant sitting room, surrounded by fine paintings, comfortable armchairs and, arranged in vases around the room, flowers from her garden. A fire glowed in the large stone hearth. Michael was struck by this direct, vibrant woman who was already an important figure in Australian public life and, from the looks of her garden, a gifted plantswoman. Perhaps they recognised something of an artist in each other then. But what neither could know was that together they would go on to create a garden famous for its beauty and warmth, built on a forty-year partnership that would prove central to both their lives.

Cruden Farm, 54 hectares (133 acres) of rolling paddocks set 56 kilometres south-east of Melbourne at Langwarrin, was given to Dame Elisabeth by her husband as a wedding gift in 1928 when she was just nineteen. The romance between the spirited young Elisabeth Greene and forty-two-year-old Sir Keith Murdoch had initially caused a society stir but it was a deeply happy union until his sudden death, aged sixty-seven, in 1952. Despite friends warning her it was too isolated, the following year his widow decided to leave Melbourne for Cruden, the home of so many happy family memories. 'People thought she was mad moving down here,' says Michael.

By the time he started work at Cruden shortly after their first cup of tea, Dame Elisabeth had been gardening there alone for two decades with not much more than casual help from semi-retired locals, who grew vegetables, raked and mowed. Edna Walling had designed the garden's early framework, including the Walled Garden, built with local stone, in the 1930s, and in following years Dame Elisabeth had planted several feature trees around the house. But it was only with Michael's arrival, and the connection of mains water soon afterwards, that the garden could begin developing as she had dreamt.

He started working at Cruden on Sunday mornings, which was then his only available time, increasing to two days a week before eventually moving up to four days a week, though he was in the garden far more often than that. Whenever his other gardening clients sold up or moved away, Dame Elisabeth asked if he could give more time to her and Cruden. 'I suggested once that she should employ someone else as well – just in case I got run over by a bus,' recalls Michael. First thing the next morning Dame Elisabeth came to find him in the garden. 'She said, "I'll risk the bus".'

He'd worked in other lovely gardens, but nothing had made an impact

TOP LEFT Keith and Elisabeth Murdoch on the front steps of Cruden.

TOP RIGHT The Murdoch family with three of their four children, (L-R) Sir Keith, Rupert, Lady Murdoch holding Anne, with Helen in front.

BOTTOM The Dame in her sitting room in 1993, where she and Michael shared their first cup of tea.

on him like Cruden, with its magnificent exotic trees and tranquil country setting – or his new employer, whose energy and charisma was infectious. The Dame lived life at a cheerful run, dashing to her car looking at her watch, carrying bunches of flowers in a bucket of water to be dropped off to friends on her way to meetings in town. She'd roar off down the drive, sometimes returning after knocking over the bucket even before she'd reached the front gate. Old George, who'd been raking and tending the vegetable garden most mornings for many years when Michael arrived, told him he couldn't bear to watch Dame Elisabeth use a kitchen knife because she chopped so terrifyingly fast. But balancing her quicksilver mind and hectic pace, says Michael, was her great gift for living thoroughly in each moment.

She expected the same effort and focus from those around her, but softened her toughness with real charm. On one of Michael's first Sundays when she found him weeding, she diplomatically mentioned that the browallia he'd been enthusiastically pulling out was in fact 'a dear friend of the garden – though it does need thinning out'. That afternoon she quietly gave him one of her plant identification books, which he studied every day over lunch. Though worn and dog-eared, he still uses it. Ideas that he or others put to her were never dismissed outright – even if her expression suggested she thought a suggestion peculiar, she would graciously take it on notice, coming back a day or so later to explain that, though a clever thought, 'it wasn't quite Cruden Farm'.

If he was instantly impressed by her, in her new gardener the Dame found a kindred spirit who shared not only the same passion for gardening but a similarly pragmatic approach to life. 'Dame Elisabeth had a wonderful spontaneous reaction to things which I don't have but she was a realist and I'm very realistic too,' explains Michael. 'I don't waste time wanting things I can't have.' Neither tolerated fools or fuss, either in people or plants, and were dismissive of their own horticultural skills. 'I'm not a great gardener although I think I might be a sensitive and felicitous one,' Dame Elisabeth told her biographer John Monks.

Both loyal, thoughtful and dogged, they shared a mischievous sense of humour, a deep appreciation of beauty and a ruthless approach to plants that had outstayed their welcome. Their like-mindedness both in and out of the garden produced not only one of Australia's greatest horticultural collaborations, but also a lifelong bond. Michael began as an employee, but ended up being like family, says Janet Calvert-Jones, one of the Dame's three daughters. 'He was so devoted to her, and she to him.'

The Dame, seen here in the 1950s, on a favourite bench in the Walled Garden, where she would often write speeches or read. 'I used to sometimes find her there sprawled out in the sun for 10 minutes', says Michael.

Thirteen years after they began shaping Cruden together, Dame Elisabeth suggested to Michael that he start keeping a diary to chart the garden's successes and schedules and record its precious rainfall. She gave him a small journal she'd bought at a local newsagency, ring-bound and coloured green and gold. On a summer's evening in 1984, he sat down at his desk and, using his favourite fountain pen, wrote the first entry of thousands in his graceful script, joined occasionally over the years by the Dame as diarist when he was away.

Sprayed roses. Dame E picked first Zinnias & tomatoes.
~ *JANUARY 7, 1984*

That inaugural diary is tentative, full of brief, self-conscious comments. Michael worried about his grammar and the spelling of plant names. But as the years passed, the diaries flourished, becoming thoughtful, frank and frequently poetic in their observations. In chronicling the garden's life, Michael hoped he was compiling a useful archive for his audience of one, who read each volume as he finished them. But what his diaries also give is a remarkable insight into the devotion of a deeply-admired public figure to the place she loved best, and into the man who worked steadfastly beside her. A lifelong bachelor absorbed by his work, those who know Michael best say he's given his all to Cruden, though he insists he has been given much in return.

Perfect weather – what a lovely time of year – but then all year perfect at Cruden Farm. ~ *FEBRUARY 12, 1991*

Even as a young boy on his family's 48-hectare (120-acre) dairy farm near Koo-Wee-Rup, south-east of Melbourne, Michael was preoccupied by plants. The second eldest of three boys and a girl, he hated being inside and often got into trouble for dawdling on his way to school. 'While my brothers wanted to be pilots or engine drivers and changed their minds every week, I always knew gardening was what I wanted to do,' he says. 'I think my father was a little horrified.'

Michael's mother, however, loved gardening and encouraged him to help her. It was a tough apprenticeship. The only water for the garden was the copper bath's soapy contents and his mother carried manure from around the farm in discarded kerosene tins to improve the soil. She coaxed camellias, roses and japonica to thrive in their small yard and grew a treasured daphne

Michael's first diary entry, written in the summer of 1984.

bush in an old bathtub. When she wanted to plant a fruit tree, she threw the family's vegetable scraps into a hole for a year before planting the young tree into the enriched soil. For her son, it was a valuable early lesson in the gardener's art of patience.

His maternal grandmother, who lived nearby, also doted on her modest garden and Michael remembers with shame how, as a child, he and his siblings popped her cherished fuchsia buds for fun. Granny Hobson, worn out from a life of hard work and regularly bedridden with heart trouble, was a forbidding figure who refused to let anyone pick her flowers – they did not, she thundered, belong inside. But knowing how keen he was, she let Michael help her weed occasionally, the boy entranced by her vivid red geraniums and the bulbs carefully planted in tins under the apple tree.

In his teens, again with his mother's encouragement, Michael began designing and making small rock gardens using pieces of granite he found on the farm, planting roses and daisies. By then the family was spending summer holidays at Seaford, a coastal hamlet on the fringe of farming land east of Melbourne. Leaving the cows in the care of a share farmer, they'd pile into the family Dodge and drive an hour to stay in a caravan parked on the block of land they'd bought, surrounded by tea-tree scrub and other families. They'd run through the dunes to the beach, where they spent hot, happy days roaming and swimming.

Just before reaching Seaford the family had to drive along Cranbourne Road – now four lanes of incessant traffic roaring through suburbia, but in those days a country road weaving across wide fields. To the impatient Morrison children, it was just another long thoroughfare on the way to holidays. But when Michael came to Cruden as an adult, he was astonished to find he remembered passing the farm's distinctive driveway of pale-skinned gums on those family trips. Though he had no idea then who lived there, it's extraordinary to think that as his teenage self sped past in the family car, just up that driveway Dame Elisabeth was already working in the garden he would dedicate his life to.

He didn't know then either how soon those dreamy summers would end. Michael's parents built a house on their beach block and were about to move there when his father died unexpectedly of a stroke, aged just forty-seven. Michael was sixteen. Four years later his beloved mother died, and in the next few years he also lost his grandparents and godmother. His sister Gay was only twelve when their mother died but, with the help of neighbours and relatives, they decided to stay in the new family home and Michael began looking after her and his younger brother, Rodney, then seventeen.

TOP The Morrison children in the backyard of their family farm in the 1950s, (L-R) Darryl, Gay, Michael and Rodney.

BOTTOM At secondary school Michael says he was a distracted student: 'I always wanted to be outside'.

12

He'd started working as a landscaper after his father's death to support the family, while studying horticulture at night, and was soon working seven days a week – a habit he kept up for decades. In his twenties he worked for a local landscaper named Jim Swanson, who remembered meeting Sir Keith and Lady Murdoch riding horses along local roads when he was a boy, and who taught his apprentice everything he knew. It was Swanson who first took Michael to Cruden to dig a well, where he briefly met Dame Elisabeth. But it wasn't until she asked nearby nursery owners Ted and Elsie Humphries, some months later, if they could recommend anyone for a gardening job that Michael's name came up. When Michael turned sixty, the Dame sent a thank you letter to the Humphries for that auspicious introduction.

From the outset there were no instructions proclaimed from the comfort of the owner's armchair at Cruden: Dame Elisabeth liked to be very much hands-on in every aspect of her life, and her garden was no exception. She and Michael were soon working side by side – shunning gloves and hats and working in all weather: in drought, mud and rain, digging, planting, weeding and watering their way through the constant cycle of seasons that lets no gardener rest for long.

Dame E and self made several attempts to work in the main border & Lilium beds – however mostly beaten by the rain & gusty winds. ~ *MARCH 5, 1985*

Dame E & I spending the morning in Rose beds – while Dame E deadheaded and removed higher black spot leaves I crawled around on all fours removing lower debris – a quick tickle up of soil with three-pronged hoe completed the work-up before lunch with Dame E. ~ *JANUARY 13, 1996*

They began sharing morning tea, brought out by Dame Elisabeth to the garden. Before long they started meeting for breakfast in the kitchen as well, often having lunch together too or sharing her afternoon teapot beside the open fire or in the shade of a favourite tree. Together they built and filled new garden beds, planted hundreds of trees, pored over plant catalogues, visited nurseries, toured overseas gardens together and readied the garden for many thousands of visitors. They would walk together around the garden most days or, in later years, go for one of their 'oo&r' trundles (named for their constant exclamations of delight)

TOP The Dame in her indispensable buggy, an 80th birthday present from her family, still used by Michael today.

BOTTOM Michael and the Dame admiring the giant liliums which filled the summer garden with scent and dramatic height.

in the Dame's electric buggy, revelling in its beauty but always watching over it intently.

> Dame E & I go for an early morning trundle – few stops on the way to deadhead & re-stake – lovely trundle from end to end enjoying the trees & undulations of the Farm. ~ *DECEMBER 19, 1999*

> Lovely early oo&r trundle with Dame E – Garden and Farm so lovely – difficult not to trundle around purring – still these rather self-indulgent trundles also give the opportunity to look and take in when relaxed – the eyes more keen to seeing pruning & staking etc. which needs attending to. ~ *NOVEMBER 17, 2000*

Right up until her death at Cruden in December 2012, at the age of 103, Dame Elisabeth lived an incredibly full life. At the heart of that rich existence was Cruden Farm, for, as Michael says, 'she loved every square inch of it, from boundary to boundary. There wasn't a plant or patch of grass that she didn't know intimately.' In him she had the extraordinary good fortune to find another gardener who came to love it just as deeply, from its oldest trees to its smallest blooms.

Despite having family in town she could stay with, the Dame would invariably make the hour's drive home after her regular evening functions in the city so she could wake up to look at the garden from her bedroom window. For his part, Michael would interrupt holidays and skip his days off to come in – ostensibly to water or check on a struggling plant but also because he so quickly missed it. Dame Elisabeth once joked that she would start charging him board. But she understood – after all, she felt the same way.

> Morning coffee with Dame E in the sun on the back Lawn – much oo&ring about the garden. ~ *SEPTEMBER 5, 1993*

> So lovely to be at Cruden to see the garden wake up after 2 days away – seems an age. ~ *SEPTEMBER 23, 2013*

As any gardener knows, gardening can be a very solitary passion, with no one as intrigued by the happenings of your garden, whether it's a city courtyard or a rural spread, as you. For the Boss and her No. 2 Gardener (as Michael still calls himself), their unwavering delight in the 8-hectare

(20-acre) garden they made was matched only by their pleasure in being able to share it for so many years with each other, both just as aware of its needs and charms, and as keen to discuss every detail of bud and leaf.

> How I miss Michael! The garden isn't quite as interesting without him. – *Dame Elisabeth* ~ SEPTEMBER 4, 1988

> Farm looks a dream – cannot wait for Dame E to see it. ~ JULY 30, 1992

Michael still lives just ten minutes' drive from Cruden, in the house his parents built. His own garden has been neglected for many years – he was, after all, always thinking of another – but at its heart is an enormous and very beautiful camellia bush, brought by his mother as a tiny plant from the family farm. In his study here, surrounded by books and photos of friends and family, he has faithfully kept the diaries, writing at night or when he wakes around 3 a.m., the camellia bush marking the passing of the years with the arrival and fading of its rich red blooms.

> Perfect weather continues. Garden rather dry. Difficult not to walk in the garden in its wonderful Autumn dress and not have a permanent smile – all so very Lovely – not a bad thing I think with our federal, state & local government ably assisted by all forms of the media working round the clock to have us in a constant state of gloom – Thank God for the garden. ~ MAY 20, 1993

He writes of the plants that have thrived and those they've lost, of terrible heat and freak storms, of escaped cows and memorable parties, carpets of golden leaves and gardening in the moonlight. The diaries recount the plans he and Dame Elisabeth hatched, the triumphs and tensions, the sheer fun of making a garden together. He tells of watching plants grow like children – the towering bay tree liberated years ago from a pot on the front doorstep, the lilac bush that came home from a church fete as a seedling in an old jam jar. In a garden without a single plant label, his encyclopaedic memory of each plant's story remains as fresh as ever.

> Over afternoon teapot with Dame E in schoolroom went over original plan for Old Fashioned Rose bed. Surprised to find it dated 1975 – how quickly time passes. ~ NOVEMBER 10, 1990

If there were ever disagreements in those many years of gardening, it was almost always about Michael's perfectionism or long hours, particularly in the busy days before a party or community event. Dame Elisabeth would often fret that he was working too hard – a case, he would retort, 'of the pot calling the kettle black'. To save her from worry – and himself from a scolding, at least until she read the diary – he would often sneak in when she was out or before she was up to get a job done.

> 4am walk on the beach, rather cool morning – breakfast then three hours at the desk. Rather missed my morning's watering at Cruden – but after our late afternoon trundle yesterday Dame E very firmly said, 'The forecast is for a mild Wednesday Michael you are not to come in'. Would much prefer 3 hours' watering than 3 hours at my desk – however nice to have the desk almost straight. 3pm Knowing Dame E was at bridge & not expected home before 6pm came out to cut round umbrella & court lawns as I want Ken to cut the back lawns in the morning – also plan to spray all lawns tomorrow afternoon. 5pm Andrew coming across the court lawn with a big smile said, One day you will get caught. *~ JANUARY 15, 2003*

> 5am – On with the watering – so pleased I came in yesterday afternoon to mow – nice to be a job ahead. *~ JANUARY 16, 2003*

As physical work became harder for her, the Dame came to rely on their partnership more and more, and even in the last year of her life, Michael was driving her around the farm, the Dame pointing out jobs which needed to be done. His devotion didn't end with her death in 2012. 'He knows just how the Dame would like this or that. Cruden is everything to him,' says ninety-year-old Frankie Farrow, a close friend of Michael's for more than half a century. He is still in the garden most days, talks of the Dame in the present tense, and feels that she is everywhere at Cruden, for where did either of them love more?

> 5am – On with the watering – what a glorious time of day to be in the garden – the birds would agree – how very fortunate I am.
> *~ NOVEMBER 10, 2002*

In an age preoccupied with selfies and spotlight chasers, with always moving on or up, Michael Morrison's diaries remind us of a different way of living – of more than forty years spent quietly but passionately dedicated to one special garden and its unique owner. Frankie Farrow tells how she and Dame Elisabeth used to sometimes hug each other and say, 'Aren't we lucky to have him!' But just as fortunate is anyone who has ever experienced Cruden's many moods and treasures, and felt the power of its rare and calming loveliness.

The spring blossom of *Cercis siliquastrum*, or Judas tree, treasured equally for its dark plum-coloured leaves in autumn.

OVERLEAF The luminous spring display of the garden's crabapples (*Malus floribunda*) with a row also espaliered and in bloom in the foreground.

CHAPTER TWO

The Two Gardeners

One of the first things Michael learnt at Cruden Farm had nothing to do with gardening. His daily cups of coffee each day were giving him headaches, he told the Dame, but tea bored him. One morning soon afterwards she appeared in the garden balancing a freshly boiled kettle and a teapot on a tray. 'I'm going to show you how to make a decent cup of tea,' she announced. Her own she drank very strong, piping hot and with great gusto, remembers Michael. 'She would drink her first cup of tea each day as though it was her first in a long time. That was how she was with life too – she enjoyed it so much.'

> Share Dame E's breakfast teapot as we discuss the placing of the four new roses. *~ JUNE 30, 2002*

They shared hundreds of cups of tea over many breakfasts at the small table in the kitchen, where they'd talk over toast with jam and, when in season, grapefruit picked from the large tree near the back door. Both early risers – the Dame thought more than four hours' sleep a lie-in – they would often meet first for a trundle or she would call Michael in from the garden where he'd already been at work for several hours. 'If I said I'd already had breakfast, she would say, "Yes, at 4 a.m.; time for your second one",' says Michael. She only let him set the table and make their breakfast once, because she'd broken her finger, and was still insisting on making it for him until she was nearly one hundred, choosing from her cupboards his favourite china, fine white crockery covered with curling tendrils of blue vine leaves.

> 7am – Dame E on her way up from the pool calls to me – breakfast in five minutes. ~ *DECEMBER 29, 2007*

The pair shared this sturdy sense of self-reliance, fostered over many years of living alone, and it is evident in the garden, as when a much-loved oak had to be moved in 1978 to stop its roots damaging the Walled Garden. With the tree held aloft by a crane, the Dame, then sixty-nine, insisted on crawling into the hole underneath the huge root-ball to secure it with hessian for the move, leaving four men, including Michael, watching on in horror. 'She said, "I couldn't bear it if anything happened to one of you",' laughs Michael. 'And we were all thinking, "Well, we're dead if something happens to you!"'

By all accounts, Dame Elisabeth was a determined and adventurous child, and she lost none of that zest with age. At eighty-two, she injured her hip climbing the grapefruit tree to prune it, at eighty-eight she was scrubbing the stable floors with a broom and hot water before functions, and she was still helping Michael rake up trailer loads of autumn leaves well into her nineties. The buggy her family gave her when she turned eighty was a favourite toy, the Dame cheerfully flooring it when going down the steep grassy banks of the sunken tennis court to shock her passengers, before roaring up to the very edge of the lake. Michael arrived early one morning to find her leaning perilously out of an upstairs window cleaning weatherboards. 'Don't you dare tell Janet!' she cried.

> Morning employed deadheading roses – nice to be out in the rain.
> 8am Over breakfast Dame E tells me she has suffered a dreadful blow – the family has asked her not to drive anymore – DE very upset as she still enjoys driving herself so much. ~ *MARCH 24, 2007*

> The Boss coming out for a trundle at 3pm – really quite hot – her nurse Sue had insisted on a large sun hat – the Boss once out of sight of the House took it off. ~ *JANUARY 20, 2011*

Dame Elisabeth, in gumboots and favourite gardening jacket, planting an oak around the new lake in 1987. 'She always said if you felt your hands in the soil, it recharged you,' says Michael.

Her extraordinary energy was matched by her indefatigable curiosity about everything and everyone. When the lake was being excavated in 1987, she would arrive home from a long day of appointments in town and head

straight down to sit on the prime mover in the dark, fascinated by its mechanics. The diaries record how at ninety-five she organised a tour of an Australia Post facility to see how mail was sorted, and Michael remembers being called in from the garden one day to watch a documentary on Western Australia's Bradshaw rock art paintings, a favourite subject. Not surprisingly, she was a reluctant patient and usually deaf to entreaties to slow down.

> Dame E meant to be resting her leg – was to be found several
> times picking off black spot leaves from the roses. ~ *JANUARY 13, 1994*

While more reserved than the Boss, Michael has his own charm – and was more than a match for Dame Elisabeth in energy and tenacity. As Janet Calvert-Jones puts it, 'My mother had a more forceful personality but Michael certainly has his own ideas and is a man of great principle – a man not for moving, as they say.' Ever humble and allergic to praise, some of Dame Elisabeth's friends nevertheless dubbed him 'Magic Michael' because he could get so much more done in the garden than mere mortals – for decades it was nothing for him to work twelve-hour days, six or seven days a week.

> 11:30am Dame E driving through on her way out for the day
> insists I go home – some helpful person had reported I have
> a cold but from the over-reaction seems I must be at death's door.
> ~ *SEPTEMBER 14, 1995*

> 2pm Dame E sent Elise out after rather heavy shower to tell me to
> go home at once – not a good idea, would have to work at my desk
> – much better to keep on with composting. ~ *SEPTEMBER 15, 1998*

With numerous philanthropic commitments ranging from the arts and education to medical research, a multitude of friends and constant visitors, Dame Elisabeth's pocket-sized red diary was always a dizzying tangle of appointments. She found it impossible to say no to anyone, but would always try to make time for the tonic of a garden trundle before heading off to yet another appointment or board meeting. Michael found her sitting in her car one evening after she'd rushed out of the house on her way to town, her head resting on the steering wheel. 'I asked if she was alright and she said, "It's absolutely the last thing I want to do, but I shall enjoy it when

I get there".' In later years, at her family's insistence, she had a driver who would take her up to town and back, often twice a day, in the unreliable old Peugeot known as No. 12, named for the numberplate on her bridal car, which the Dame used on every subsequent car she owned.

> A perfect autumn day – enjoyed working in the garden with
> Dame E this afternoon – the past month has been so very
> busy – with commitments in town and overseas visitors to the
> garden – six couples in the past two days alone. ~ *MARCH 30, 1990*

> Dame E's days seem to become fuller with each passing week –
> her first appointment of the morning 8.45am – we just manage to
> squeeze in a quick buggy tour of the garden – so pleased with the
> roses & Homeless Plants bed – arriving back at the House for
> Dame E's first appointment – two in all before her lunch guests
> – Dame E then leaving 4.50pm for two functions in town – too
> much for No. 12 which blew its radiator at Cranbourne Rd rounda-
> bout – Dame E & Don continuing on in Don's van. ~ *OCTOBER 28, 1997*

Having seen plenty of gardens that have cost a fortune to design but feel cold and charmless, Michael is sure that the most engaging are those in which the owner remains involved, both emotionally and practically, in its daily life. It meant a great deal to him that no matter how busy she was or how preoccupied she seemed, Dame Elisabeth never lost touch with her garden.

> Continue clean-up of roses from Tuesday – pleased to find three
> lovely tidy heaps of diseased material on paths collected by Dame
> E since Tuesday between her busy appointments. ~ *FEBRUARY 12, 1987*

> Dame E left early for another hectic day in town but not before
> collecting me from the native patch to go for oo&r drive around
> the lake in her car – during which it was decided to add some more
> of our local eucalypts in the paddock immediately behind the lake
> – existing trees going out at a great rate. ~ *MAY 31, 1990*

Two mornings a week for twenty-nine years, until 2012, the Dame's secretary, Judy Watts, arrived at Cruden to work with the Boss at her study table among stacks of reports and correspondence. 'The mail she received

every day was inches high, and together we sent out at least thirty letters a day,' says Judy. On one typical day when she was ninety-eight, the Dame had a lunch meeting, took posies to two friends in hospital in the afternoon and presented an award in the evening at the Victorian College of the Arts in town – even so, the garden's latest change was foremost in her mind.

> DE coming to cheer Ken & I on in Old Fashioned Rose bed
> before leaving for lunch appointment saying she could not bear
> to leave for the day before looking again at the improved air space
> & balance of Rose bed. ~ *MARCH 15, 2007*

Michael held the fort when she was away, his loyalty and skill providing the crucial ballast to the constant demands that kept her from the garden far more than she liked. But he missed her company and advice, and worried for her too.

> Turn pots of lilium around in the Hope they might grow straight
> – what a job – not my favourite – so difficult to decide which to
> dump – several pots past their best – miss Dame E's strong-minded
> back up. ~ *NOVEMBER 12, 1992*

> Quite dark by 5pm – worried Dame E not Home. ~ *MAY 31, 1994*

For her part, the Boss lamented that she missed too much of the fun. Leaving for town one day, she found Michael catching fish while cleaning out the Walled Garden pond; she was soon in the water in her stockings wanting to help. If she noticed something new in the garden as she was heading out, she'd race to fetch her camera, clambering through the beds for the perfect shot. She'd emerge dishevelled and exclaim, 'Can't be helped!' before brushing herself down and hurrying off.

As enthusiastic as they were about it, Dame Elisabeth and Michael avoided being extravagant in the garden. They were thrifty in the best sense of the word, both from childhoods where money was often tight. The Dame flew economy when she travelled and told Michael she felt sick when her family booked her a business-class seat. She was particularly horrified when an Archbishop arrived for afternoon tea in a limousine. Her gifts were thoughtful but rarely new – perhaps one of her own books or prints – wrapping held in place by a ribbon so it could be reused. It was a shared ethos that made them wonderfully resourceful in the garden,

The Dame's favourite spot in the Walled Garden beside the fish pond, under the branches of an old crabapple – one of the few trees left from the original Edna Walling plantings.

where many plants have been grown from cuttings or collected seed. 'Some people have said over the years, "Yes, she has a lovely garden but of course she can afford to",' says Michael, who still uses budding tape retrieved from plants to tie up posies. 'But it didn't come from money, it came from hard work.'

> Sowed *Eucalyptus maculata* seed which Dame E and I collected on our plantation crawl – seed was then left in a dish in front of the hall fire until the seed pods burst – we hope to be able to grow the trees for the new drive. ~ *JULY 21, 1990*

Michael has never forgotten overhearing a guest to the house after the Dame's death sniff, 'How shabby it is; she must have been very mean.' Anyone who knew of her enormous donation of time and money to charitable causes, attended one of her famous parties or knew how much she spent each year on tree maintenance would know better. The reason she kept her faded curtains was not stinginess, but because she and Sir Keith chose them together – for beneath that composed exterior lay a romantic who never remarried and never forgot the great love of her life. What's more, she didn't see the point of endless new possessions, whether it was furniture or cars. 'She knew the garden had to change to stay the same but she didn't believe in change for change's sake,' says Michael. 'She kept everything special by not overindulging.'

Hence there are no statements of status at Cruden, no vaulted ceilings or marble floors. The house is filled with old and lovely furniture but, like the curtains, the carpets have seen better days and the effect is of much-loved comfort rather than self-conscious grandeur. Dame Elisabeth herself used to call it 'that funny old place' – the garden was to her far more precious. The room she spent most time in, the schoolroom, so named because her children had lessons there when they lived at Cruden during the Second World War, has her simple round study table and three mismatched armchairs gathered around the fireplace. Shelves are crammed with books, walls with paintings and everywhere are photos of family and friends. Like the house, it is a room of ineffable warmth and charm.

Both the house and garden reflected its owner for, despite her many personal achievements and accolades, Dame Elisabeth remained resolutely unpretentious, treating everyone, whether she was meeting a prime minister or school children, the same. One afternoon as she carried boxes out to her car, Jack Goudie, an elderly man who raked in the garden for years and was

The Boss was always delighted to see children roaming the garden – 'she loved their laughter and their energy,' says Michael.

devoted to the Dame, leapt to help her, asking cryptically, 'Why bark, milady, when you have dogs?' Taken aback only for a moment, she shot back with a smile, 'Because, Jack, I like to bark with the dogs.' As with many other tales of the Boss, it's one Michael tells with much amusement.

> Dame E spent the early morning before leaving for town cleaning her car – also some running repairs on the roof having climbed out of an upstairs window. ~ *APRIL 12, 1988*

An excursion when the ninety-year-old Dame asked Michael to drop her at a formal event in the city, before he collected some plants at a nursery, summed up her straightforward approach to life:

> Wish I had thought to bring the camera – as we draw up at 81 Collins St, with several very smartly dressed ladies being dropped off in smart cars at the Alexandra Club – Dame E leaping out of the ute with evening clothes over her arm. ~ *JULY 13, 1999*

Michael is the same, for while Cruden has attracted many well-known guests over the years, he's never starstruck – in his diaries, famous visitors (whether art patrons, political leaders or distinguished actors) are mentioned without fanfare, and he himself always assiduously avoided the spotlight.

> Garden looking a dream – weather very promising – among Dame E's lunch guests today the Rex Harrisons and Claudette Colbert – all reported to be garden lovers. ~ *NOVEMBER 2, 1986*

> I was asked would I be agreeable to come round the garden on camera and answer some questions. No – my usual answer – Dame Elisabeth Murdoch's the owner of Cruden Farm – Dame Elisabeth's the designer, maker and head gardener. ~ *OCTOBER 2, 2003*

What counts when he meets someone is not how acclaimed they are or how many botanical names they can recite but simply how much they enjoy being in the garden – in Michael's opinion, plants know when they're in the presence of an admirer. 'If you really want to grow a plant you love in your garden you should try three times,' he advises. 'Plants make up their own mind if they know they're loved.' He and Dame Elisabeth both admitted defeat, however, when it came to gardenias. 'Gardenias have never liked me and when Dame E was given two as a gift I said, "I'm not touching them – they'll die for sure",' says Michael. 'The Boss said, "They don't like me either".' One did indeed die, and as for the other, 'I just look the other way when I walk past it.'

A distrust of gardenias was just one of many gardening traits they had in common – from possessing the same eye for space and light in the garden to measuring rainfall with almost religious fervour and having the same thought about the garden at the same time.

> At 8am breakfast DE suggests perhaps Ken & I might clear out holding bed below apple tree & prune pear & apple – have begun – so often the case when either DE or I suggest a job at breakfast the other has had it in mind to do so. ~ *JUNE 23, 2005*

When he first began at Cruden, Michael would disappear into the garden when the Murdoch family arrived. 'That's the way we were brought up to work in the garden,' he says. 'If they were there you got things done and then faded into the background.' But he's become very close to many of her children and grandchildren too, joining them for regular lunches, family days and celebrations. 'He's one of my very favourite people,' says Penny Fowler, one of the Dame's twenty grandchildren. For Michael the health and happiness of the garden, and of its Head Gardener and her family, were always inseparable.

> Worth reporting encounter with Master Keith Handbury – briefly interrupted his fishing excursion in the Walled Garden fish pond… when he saw me deadheading the Anthemis – looking quite serious said "Michael, Great-Granny will be cross if you cut off all her flowers" – reassuring to see the fourth generation taking such an interest in Cruden Farm. ~ *JANUARY 8, 1985*

> Lake level up to just below cottage stormwater pipe again – Dame E much stronger each day. ~ *FEBRUARY 6, 1988*

> Great excitement with 3 blooms on the tree gardenia at end of Picking Garden – the first blooms this plant has produced ever. Dame E pleased with her visit to specialist – very good report – cleared to drive her car. ~ *MARCH 30, 1998*

The diaries chart the milestones of their friendship, the Dame's comings and goings, and the family successes and celebrations, just as attentively as they do the garden's happenings. Above all, they reveal how much the pair enjoyed each other's company, in and out of the garden.

> Michael did all the necessary jobs before his departure on his Gardens tour – I shall miss him sorely – what little I can do in the garden is so much more enjoyable when shared with him – but I shall comfort myself in his absence by thinking and hoping that he will be having a richly deserved and very enjoyable trip. – *Dame Elisabeth*. ~ *APRIL 29, 1988*

> 9.20am Help Dame E to pack picnic baskets into car – setting off rather like a day on our UK jaunts with Dame E navigating – stopping a little way from Lambley Nursery to picnic under the shade of a cypress tree – weather and countryside perfect – after delicious chicken & salad, fresh fruit picnic lunch prepared by Dame E ready to go on… Set off home 5.15pm – whiskey and soda with Dame E in drawing room – end to a most pleasant day.
> ~ *FEBRUARY 21, 1999*

In one of her turns as diarist Dame Elisabeth describes Michael as 'a tower of strength as usual', and at the heart of their great friendship was this certainty that she could depend on him for anything, but especially to care for Cruden just as she did. As she said to him on more than one occasion as they walked among its flowers and trees, 'Michael, I trust you to look after our garden.'

Michael in the serene oasis
of the Walled Garden.

CHAPTER THREE

The Trees

Collect remainder of the leaves – garden so lovely – with all the warmth & tracery of the trees & winter wood – do love this time of year – really shows up the form and bones of the garden – such warmth and strength. Dame E walking in the garden – delaying leaving for the day until the last possible moment – saying how she hates leaving all this beauty – even just for the day.

~ JULY 5, 1993

From the moment you turn into Cruden Farm's modest entrance, it is the trees that mesmerise. First is the long front drive, that sinuous tunnel of more than one hundred lemon-scented gums planted by Dame Elisabeth and Sir Keith in 1929. Their clean fragrance spices the air and when streaked with rain their pale-pink wood gleams like soft moonlight. At dawn most days Michael walks, as he has for many years, past the two enormous elms that watch over the sleeping house and down this winding avenue to open the wooden front gates. He loves his solitary stroll as the garden wakes, never tiring of the shape of the smooth trunks, the glimpses of paddocks between them or the dance of leaves overhead.

6am – So enjoy my early morning walk down front drive to open gates. Elm blossom framing front of the house – so very special.

~ SEPTEMBER 15, 2013

Dame Elisabeth in the avenue she and Sir Keith planted nearly a century ago. She always encouraged visitors to walk among the sleek trunks.

OVERLEAF With its ever-changing play of light and shade, the drive is today an icon of Australian gardening.

It's fitting that trees welcome you to Cruden given how central they have always been in Dame Elisabeth's vision for it. When Michael arrived in 1971, the Dame had already planted several of the main trees in the inner garden, including the magnificent copper beech planted close to the house in memory of her husband. Together the pair would go on to plant hundreds more trees as the garden expanded under their care, delighting in the their growth and eagerly finding room for more, always mindful of the balance of space and air between them, selecting each tree for the way its bark, foliage and form could enhance the landscape around it.

Wonderful vista from stable yard, looking across lawn to house & stone walls – silver birches – elms and oaks in autumn. Wonderful. Standing on top landing of new steps with Dame E – both made suggestions as to what special tree might be planted beyond dams as background to vista – failed to make a choice. ~ *MAY 17, 1986*

More than any other plant, trees define the garden's structure across the seasons, their colours and textures linking one part of the garden to another, providing sculpture or shade, softening buildings and sharp corners, and giving the garden much of its personality of age and strength. Each has its own purpose and charm. A tree's height may complement or accentuate that of its neighbours, its autumn foliage might colour sooner or later, and its shape contrast with the form of trees nearby or gently remind you of trees in another part of the garden. It is a complex choreography that the two gardeners knew succeeds best when it appears effortless.

Plant five silver poplars – should make nice winter bones – also their grey wood compatible with local gum colour. ~ *JUNE 25, 1988*

Dame E marked the site of a second Oak – in time will be lovely company to its parents across the bridge. ~ *NOVEMBER 3, 1992*

Some trees have been planted to frame vistas or shimmer at the end of them – hints of treasures further on. Together they give the garden its harmony and depth as the eye is drawn irresistibly from one layer of colour, branch or leaf to the next.

While on our oo&r buggy ride yesterday Dame E and I discovered, while looking back to the house from the Erwin Fabian

The tri-colour beech near the house, from which Michael used to often collect foliage for vases by climbing onto the roof.

OVERLEAF Dawn suffuses the columns of *Corymbia maculata*, planted to echo the columns of the house, with a wood carving by assistant gardener Ken Blum, 'Dryad – The Spirit of the Trees', in the foreground.

sculpture, the Macedon oak – moved some years ago on the back lawn – has grown so tall it's now possible to see its autumn colour over the house & English oak. We often say if you take the time you see something new every day – How true. ~ APRIL 24, 1994

Stopping across the lake overflow to look back at the rich tapestry of foliage surrounding the house with young beech foliage, ghost maples and spring greens – one of Dame E's favourite vistas – collecting sweet peas – roses – forget-me-not & polyanthus as we return through the Picking Garden. ~ OCTOBER 2, 2001

As much as he loves the garden's flowers, for Michael they are always secondary: 'The trees are the main thing.' They are, he says, what drew him to Cruden in the first place. 'What I missed in the younger gardens I made and worked on was established trees.' Throughout his diaries those trees vividly chart the seasons – the hawthorns aglow with autumn berries, the winter lattice of bare wood, rich in age and texture, the eruption in spring of the crabapples into fairy floss blossom, and the deep wells of canopy shade that cool the garden in summer.

Lovely green blossom on Elms – lovely new growth of the willows – soft lush fresh yellow green – all so full of promise – cannot believe how quickly the wood of the golden basket willows lose their rich gold wood of winter & go to green yellow – within a week of breaking into leaf. ~ SEPTEMBER 15, 1991

Prunus mume in full bloom filling the garden with its lovely sweet drifting perfume. ~ JULY 30, 1996

Today the first Pin Oak just past Lake overflow bridge shows a little Autumn colour at the very top – this tree always the first to begin turning. ~ APRIL 4, 2013

The winter silhouette of one of the garden's magnificent oaks, framed by the pencil pines and the stables, with glints of water in the distance.

OVERLEAF Michael rakes in the shade of the old weeping elm, the centrepiece for several of the Dame's memorable party marquees.

Even more than their seasonal changes, Michael respects their deep-rooted strength, so dramatically on show in their winter forms. 'They make you feel things can't be as bad as they appear to be in the world,' he says, one hand on the trunk of a towering poplar, its grey bark puckered like gathered fabric, looking more pillar than plant. One of the trees planted by Dame Elisabeth to subdue the three-storey white house she

found so overbearing in her early days at Cruden, it rises like an obelisk over a sea of green lawn.

Early morning walk round the lake across the Barn paddock to check the Leylandii plantation… with luck this plantation will be a wonderful asset – adding extra form to the garden – What a treat – as I turned to retrace my steps across the hill – the most marvellous view of the stables, house & garden (wish Dame E was with me) through the golden wood of the willows – lovely group of paperwhites in bloom – across the water the marvellous orange gold of the two Barn oaks – such wonderful colour with the stone of the stables – the lighter green of the citrus and fruit & one marvellous *Acacia baileyana* in corner of the Walled Garden – the warmth, strength and tracery of the Elm and Oak and Birches – the form of pencil pines and Torulosa through the deciduous trees – what a sight. ~ *JULY 9, 1989*

Early morning inspection of Monday planting – Eucalypts standing straight & strong – such a marvellous feeling having these trees in. ~ *MAY 2, 1991*

The mingling of native and exotic, of gum and wattle with beech and cypress, has been achieved through much thought and constant reassessment by the two gardeners. The result is a brilliant melding of the garden and its collection of exotic specimen trees tapering off into the very Australian paddocks and bush beyond. No one tree is allowed to dominate – it's quite deliberate that the immense blue gum planted many years ago in front of the house to begin the progression there from garden to bush is matched in stature by the elms nearby, while the creamy late winter blooms of the large michelia in the Picking Garden are quietened by the milky waves of jonquils flowering across the lake at the same time. 'Never a jarring note was one of the Boss' constant sayings,' says Michael. 'She didn't like show-offs in the garden.'

Dame E prefers to plant en masse with one variety so that trees flow in a strong picture. ~ *AUGUST 28, 1993*

Dame E suggests we might add 2–4 more Nyssa to group – three a little self-conscious. ~ *MAY 2, 1999*

Cruden's ghost maple, the calming tones of its variegated foliage bringing a sense of lightness and coolness to the garden.

Just as they link different parts of the garden, and the garden with the farm, so Cruden's trees are a living connection with its past. Many trees feature in its long history – from the walnut tree grown from a nut given to Dame Elisabeth and the maple planted to mark the grave of her beloved dog Lily, to the vast gum that the Dame brought home from a holiday as a seed wrapped in a tissue. And every spring as the elms on the round lawn in front of the house burst into lime-green blossom, she reminded Michael that the flowers were falling the day Sir Keith died.

As he passes the wooden table under the copper beech Michael remembers his many morning teas with the Boss there on Sundays after she'd been to church. The three poplars beside the lake, their silver leaves fluttering in the breeze like butterfly wings, came as cuttings from a friend's garden, while the weeping elm reminds him of the grand parties held long ago in tents specially erected to enclose the old tree as its centrepiece. With Michael as keeper of their stories, these and other trees chronicle the garden's many chapters of friendship and loss.

> We also placed the Myer Oak – gift from the Ken Myers on Dame E's 80th – grown from an acorn from his mother's tree.
> ~ *NOVEMBER 9, 1989*

> Sad day at Cruden Farm with the passing of our lovely Lily this morning. Dame E has decided to lay Lily to rest in the cottage garden just below French doors – we have planted a lovely maple to mark her place. ~ *MARCH 7, 1995*

> *Prunus spinosa* showing more bloom today – DE suggests we use some in the house flowers with John & Margaret Chandler coming to lunch on Tuesday – John grew the Prunus especially for Dame E some 30–35 years ago. ~ *AUGUST 26, 2001*

There are few greater pleasures at Cruden than sitting under an oak like this one, which began life as an acorn taken from the country garden of the Dame's sister, the late Sylvia Ritchie.

OVERLEAF Looking back towards the house over the lake, the ornamental pear *Pyrus ussuriensis* in riotous spring leaf.

The Dame treasured such long connections and always invited those coming to work in the garden to plant trees as a way of beginning new ones. Michael clearly remembers his own first saplings – three appropriately hardy ironbarks now prospering in a dark-trunked cluster near the stables. The extended Murdoch clan has taken root here too, with each of Dame Elisabeth's daughters and granddaughters planting their own tree over the years, greeted by Michael on a walk through the garden simply as 'Lizzie's Ginkgo' or 'Penny's Nyssa'.

This tree doubly important as not only Katie's tree but
chestnut grown from a seed collected by Andrew P. from
a Belgium Arboretum and given to Dame E three years ago.
~ *NOVEMBER 23, 1996*

Trees are cherished too at Cruden for protecting its sense of seclusion from
the busy suburbs that have steadily consumed surrounding rural proper-
ties. Now overseen by John Christie, who joined Cruden's garden team in
2011 and became its first general manager in 2013, tracts of bush on the
farm are being regenerated with indigenous trees such as peppermint
gums, black wattles, banksias and casuarinas to resemble the area's original
heath and swamp woodland vegetation. These native species join more
than 4000 trees that have been planted over the past few decades to create
dense barriers of leaf along the farm's boundaries.

Afternoon spent with Dame E planting 7 new *Acacia prominens* at
bottom of native plantation – hope to deaden some of the traffic
noise. ~ *NOVEMBER 3, 1984*

Early morning spent with Dame E checking staking of young
trees around lake while Tom went on to clear grass from around
their roots – Dame E and I went on to look at site for new pine
plantation to screen new housing estate north side. ~ *AUGUST 23, 1988*

Finally begin planting the new plantation to block out new freeway
beginning with double row of *Eucalyptus maculata* – 32 in all –
Dame E very pleased. ~ *OCTOBER 26, 2010*

The special and varied role trees play in the making of Cruden's mood and
beauty is reflected in the constant attention they're given. Michael is astonished when people assume that trees can be left to fend for themselves soon
after planting – under his stewardship trees are fed, sprayed, watered and
pruned. 'The Boss considered it a waste of a tree not to give it some help,'
he says.

Young trees are watered diligently for their first three years, and remain
a priority in dry times. In the early years, before Dame Elisabeth found
a tree surgeon she trusted, she and Michael always took holidays at different
times in case a special tree was damaged and a decision had to be made
quickly on its future.

Most satisfying day spent with Dame E pruning citrus fruit (death and destruction) – reduced lemon trees by a third – had become much too heavy in foliage, also good deal of dead wood.
~ *SEPTEMBER 10, 1984*

Wet miserable morning – top dress around crabapples by lake cottage steps with fowl manure – rather let them down last season as a result did not get the new growth I had hoped for. ~ *JUNE 17, 1989*

Pruning, whether for a tree's wellbeing or the garden's composition, is a job demanding an understanding of not only the garden's evolution but also of its future. Being too hasty is as risky as being too slow. 'Trees may be slow growing but you can still miss your chance with them,' says Michael. When a new assistant gardener takes it upon himself to cut back a tree, he gets some gentle advice.

With tact I hope told him we just do not rip into trees without first consulting Dame E – as she has an eye for the trees in the four seasons. ~ *FEBRUARY 19, 1990*

While Dame Elisabeth prided herself on thrift and self-reliance in many areas of her life, she invested in regular tree surgery to keep her trees as resilient as possible, removing weak or suspect limbs, watching for sickness and coaxing more life out of aging favourites. Melbourne arborist Tom Greenwood began visiting Cruden more than thirty years ago to help care for its trees. 'The Dame absolutely loved every tree and Michael has such a sense of custodianship for the garden,' he says.

4pm Really the most frightening hour of gale force winds – had thought at the peak we would lose the elms – However the tree work done over the years stood by us – very little real damage – just a great deal of light debris – though several trees down on the Farm. ~ *AUGUST 5, 1991*

Once again feel very grateful that Dame E has had so much maintenance done on the large trees these last 20 years – feel sure as I walk around the garden we would have had more serious damage – as it is no large limbs down in the garden just good deal of foliage & debris. ~ *JANUARY 3, 1995*

OVERLEAF Bare wood disappears in an explosion of elm and cherry blossom.

But the diaries tell too of those times when more elemental forces won out, such as the spring day in 1999 when a freak storm hit. 'We just heard a noise and the storm came roaring up the drive,' recalls Michael. 'It didn't last long but it blew the *Prunus spinosa* out of the Grey border, we lost two Chinese beauty bushes and a ceanothus and then it came round the corner and blew the gum out of the ground. The garden looked like it hadn't been raked in months.'

It was not until Dame E had left for the day that I set out round the lake to check how we had come through the storm – Horror – to find the beautiful old Eucalypt on the point of the peninsula – a natural sculpture – had gone over roots and all into the water – so sad – pleased Dame E had not gone for her last look round the lake before leaving as she so often does – would have spoilt her day – bad news can wait – we often say in hindsight these things are for the best – but do not think in this case will be so – impossible to repeat the wonderful leaning form of the tree – remainder of the day rather difficult to get moving. ~ *SEPTEMBER 16, 1999*

Disease, drought and gales always made the two gardeners anxious, and they mourned every tree they lost.

During a brief lull in the wind we all heard a crack then almost instantly a crash – good half of the large liquidambar at top of Picking Garden steps down on drive & Lawns – thank God today & not Sunday as am sure several people would have been hurt. Dame E in town this afternoon so she will be saved hearing the news until the morning. ~ *FEBRUARY 27, 2007*

Arrive to debris down in front drive lawns but so much worse to come as I drive to stables – drive back of stables blocked – the wonderful *Eucalyptus rubida* has fallen over roots & all into stables – a great loss… Such sad news to give Dame E who planted it as a very young plant over seventy years ago. ~ *SEPTEMBER 5, 2010*

Michael still misses that white-trunked candlebark's graceful bulk looming protectively over the stables. But while he and Dame Elisabeth thought of such trees as 'dear friends', they could also be ruthless, as all good gardeners must be. With the pair regularly appraising each tree's contribution to the garden's overall picture, each mature tree at Cruden today has earnt its right to be there many times over.

> Avocado tree for the chop – given two years over its promised
> fruiting time – nothing done – replaced with large conifer. ~ MAY 7, 1985

> Sad morning – time has come – five years of unsuccessful tree
> surgery & root drenching with fungicides trying everything
> possible to restore standard Mt Fuji outside dining room windows
> to health have failed – so the decision has been made to harden our
> hearts – to remove and start again – Dame E has Martin here to
> help me with the dreaded job. ~ MAY 11, 1985

> Last week Dame E decided it was time to end the tree's struggle
> – sad especially as the tree had been a gift from the late Mrs Cook.
> ~ APRIL 30, 1992

Some decisions were especially hard, such as the removal of the ailing 'Mt Fuji', an old flowering cherry tree that was so breathtaking in spring that Dame Elisabeth for many years held a celebratory lunch when its blossom was framed by the dining-room windows. The loss was made even harder by the knowledge that neither of them would live long enough to see its replacement in maturity. But most choices were soon vindicated, as when the pair decided to remove several trees, including a sixty-five-year-old *Corymbia ficifolia*.

> As I drive in cannot believe the improvement with the removal of
> trees from pool area on Thursday – Air balance & flow so much
> better – structural picture of stable garage buildings coming down
> the slope of the Lawn to design of Walled Garden so much better
> without these trees – Rather nervous of approaching the stone
> bridge where the ficifolia near the flat veranda was so important to
> the picture – but as so often the case – I feel rather disloyal to say
> do not miss the tree at all – in fact prefer the view of the house
> without it. ~ MARCH 9, 1996

Preserving that precious balance of light and space, while at the same time allowing for each tree's growth and preparing for its eventual decline, was always their desire.

OVERLEAF The mesmerising reflections of the two ornamental pears by the lake, with a view to the trees of the outer paddocks between them.

The most wonderful productive oo&r buggy ride with Dame E all over garden – Lake area and garden plantations – Dame E marking good many trees for the chop – beginning with the *Prunus mume* in Grey & White border – we both love this tree in bloom but really is much too large for position – Mt Fuji in Lilium bed & so on we go – one possibly two old Birches at pool walk – Prunus pool steps – really all well past their best – finishing in the pool plantation several to go there – a very productive morn – Dame E has such a good eye for the future – scale – air & balance.
~ *MARCH 2, 1996*

Dame E coming to cheer us on – as often the case when a plant or tree goes out – really the picture is better without – time had come for more light & air – more sky. ~ *APRIL 3, 2000*

Keen foresight and much patience are needed to create a garden with trees. No plant speaks more of the future than a young tree, and with their unhurried growth and long lives, trees embody gardeners at their most generous and optimistic, planting so often for another generation's pleasure rather than their own.

Rather missing the large pines from Barn Hill – find myself looking up – all the extra light – the form and age of these old trees – still will be nice to get on with the young trees for the future. ~ *MARCH 30, 1994*

Take the lower limbs off Oaks in Gate House area – after some inspection Ken and I decide trees need taking up to a height of 8–10 Ft – Dame E hopeful that in the future visitors to open days will find it a pleasant area for picnics – saving visitors carrying their baskets too far. ~ *AUGUST 8, 2002*

After morning coffee Ken and I walk round lake looking at young Oak trees deciding which lower limbs can be taken off this winter – Dame E and I had discussed this on our Sunday trundle – both aware how important to keep an eye on the structure of young trees for the future – Dame E always anxious not to completely overgrow the lake – a few of the Oaks we are able to allow to stay branched to the ground – but most must be trunked up to at least 12 feet for the future. ~ *AUGUST 11, 2009*

Of the more than seventy oaks Michael has helped plant, most are now adults and large enough to shelter under; strong, bright towers sketched in reflections on the lake. 'The Boss always felt that oaks stood by you, if you got them off to a good start,' he says. He finds it enormously rewarding to watch the trees he planted with her finally come into their own.

> One of those lovely misty autumn mornings I love – could not resist the temptation of an oo&r walk before making a start. Autumn leaves this season have given us great pleasure – think particularly as some of the young trees planted in the last ten years and less are now large enough to claim their place in the overall picture… a lovely heavy mist giving the Farm an air of mystery – patches of clear giving wonderful reflection of the gold autumn birches – Macedon Oak – elms & liquidambar. ~ *MAY 27, 1990*

He shared that delight with Dame Elisabeth, whose enthusiasm for the trees never waned, even after more than eighty years of planting.

> Mid-afternoon having seen her Children's Hospital guests off Dame E came to say she had 45 Minutes before changing to leave for town and would love a trundle to place group of Eucalypts on mound across lake. ~ *APRIL 30, 2001*

> Dame E anxious to do some serious tree planting this year. ~ *APRIL 18, 2009*

> Make a run for nursery – the Boss had suggested during Sunday's drive round outer garden adding another 3 *Pyrus ussuriensis* to the 2 at barn end of Lake as Pyrus are our first good autumn colour for the year. ~ *APRIL 14, 2011*

As the years passed in their cycle of bare branch and new leaf, Cruden's trees have never been far from the two gardeners' thoughts. When the Dame came home after a hospital stay late in that last year of her life, it was the trees they both looked for:

> Elm trees in full bloom – wisteria lovely over schoolroom – late morning the Boss & Barb arrive home in ambulance – the Boss pleased to see the trees in the drive through the windows. ~ *OCTOBER 1, 2012*

OVERLEAF Among the many moods of Cruden, a sense of deep tranquillity is its most powerful.

63

CHAPTER FOUR

The Winter Garden

Stoke hall fire – icy wind – lovely clear winter sky – garden a dream – continue pruning – 4.30 afternoon tea with Dame E by schoolroom fire – pruning of Picking Garden roses almost complete. *~ JULY 1, 2003*

A bitter breeze gusts across the rose beds where Michael has been pruning for several hours since early morning. Despite the cold and the thorns, his weathered hands are bare – he never wears gloves, preferring the familiar feel of stem and soil. As he moves expertly among the leafless bushes, he watches ducks scatter silver ripples as they hurry across the lake. The sharp outlines of bare trees are like etchings on its dark surface, and the spent red leaves of their autumn finery crackle underfoot. The wind irritates his asthmatic cough, and his days in the winter garden begin and often end in chilly darkness, yet this remains his very favourite of seasons.

Temp 15 – Glorious clear morning – perfect reflections in the lake – every leaf & twig of the willows reflected in the water.
~ JUNE 15, 1989

Quite lunch time before I was able to feel my hands – getting soft in my old age. *~ JUNE 19, 1997*

Though he appreciates summer's festive parade as much as any gardener, Michael relishes winter as a time of quieter pleasures, whether it's the

The two gardeners planted thousands of winter-flowering bulbs around the lake to celebrate their favourite season.

OVERLEAF The bare golden branches of the basket willows bring warmth on a cold winter's day.

delicate snowflake-like blooms covering the *Camellia lutchuensis* or the drifts of shy hellebores, their pink and green faces turned to the ground. Occasionally he arrives to find Cruden glittering with frost or cloaked with fog, the skeletal trees looming through the shadows with eerie loveliness. On such days, the farm feels more sealed off than ever from the restless streets around it.

Breeze quite icy – Fuji cherry *Prunus incisa* 'Praecox' flowering and giving pleasure the last few weeks with its lovely lacy blossom – at this minute at its peak – Dame E and I stopping to soak in its beauty. ~*JUNE 23, 2001*

Rich gold of the Elms with their golden carpet on the Round lawn light the early morning through the fog as I arrive – I shall miss their warm welcome when all the leaves have fallen. ~*JUNE 21, 2003*

Even after autumn's radiance, Michael prefers winter's more subtle palette, especially the many bark colourings of the garden's deciduous trees, with their markings and murals of lichen. As he walks the garden he notices the myriad textures – from the grey-limbed pin oaks around the lake, their spindly fingers just touching the water, to the copper beech, its trunk wrinkled like elephant hide, and the smooth sheen of the lemon-scented gums, with bulges like sinew beneath their taut skin. Silvery snail tracks glisten up and down a flowering cherry, the ridges of its bark raised like ribs.

The bones of the garden so clear at this time of year… feel I want to walk people round garden & farm at this time and share – How very lucky I am to be here. ~*AUGUST 30, 1992*

Taking Lily for her early walk to the barn yard found on turning back to the garden the most wonderful picture – with the early sun rising through the golden wood of the basket willows lighting up the bulbs & lake in the most wonderful soft light. ~*AUGUST 27, 1994*

The *Magnolia denudata* in its winter glory sets off the dark wood of the copper beech, the giant tree planted by the Dame in memory of her husband.

OVERLEAF, LEFT Michael pruning Cruden's roses – a winter ritual he and the Boss spent many hours on each year together.

OVERLEAF, RIGHT The Picking Garden, pruned and tilled, sleeps until spring.

There are plenty of gardeners who dread winter as little more than a grey waiting room for spring. But even after more than forty winters at Cruden, Michael still delights in the meditative stillness of frosty mornings and the beds of freshly dug-over soil, the overcast sky reflected in the lake, and the scents of daphne and garrya on the crisp air. Above all, he loves the winter

garden's simplicity, its architecture laid bare and the shapes of the deciduous trees like sculptures. It's his season for contemplating the elemental joys of space and light.

> Garden looking wonderful showing all its winter bones – full of strength and promise. ~ *AUGUST 10, 1985*

> Late afternoon light carries the garden & lake area into dream time – Hard to leave and go home. ~ *JULY 17, 1993*

Softening the shapes of the bare trees, like splashes of sunlight at their feet, jostle crowds of jonquils, snowdrops, paperwhites and many types of daffodils. Crucial in this picture are the evergreens, particularly the citrus trees, whose glossy foliage is hidden under an enormous crop of limes, lemons and oranges – Dame Elisabeth couldn't stand to see them rotting on the ground and gave away boxes of fruit to friends and local nursing homes each year. Their colours are repeated in the thousands of bright bulbs around the lake, and in the many wattles planted to ring the outer garden like a garland of gold.

> Afternoon most unpleasant – However not possible to feel miserable with the weather when at a glance in any direction the Farm full of warm sunny blossom from the Acacia – the cottage & Lake area just awash with daffs – *Prunus spinosa* & cherry plum a dream. ~ *AUGUST 27, 1996*

> Acacias & bulbs wonderful – Dame E keeps saying 'I wish everyone could enjoy them'. ~ *AUGUST 30, 2005*

Every day Michael inspects the magnolia trees, hoping the possums have spared the fattening buds of blossom. He loves the striking effect of these goblet-like flowers on their bare branches, and waits eagerly for the scarlet blooms to appear on the cinnamon-coloured limbs of the Persian ironwood tree, *Parrotia persica*, its knobbly trunk covered in glistening spider webs. Every winter, when this unusual tree was briefly in bloom, the Dame cut a few branches to fill a favourite Chinese vase in the front hall. 'She felt you had to make an effort to discover it,' says Michael, 'otherwise it was gone in a minute.'

Winter's myriad highlights in the garden include radiant notes of citrus, wattle and the texture of mossy trunks. In an oak tree a nest sits empty until spring.

Dame E going for oo&r drive round the Lake & down the back drive on her way to early church – arrived back saying she had fallen in love with the Farm all over again. ~JULY 11, 1993

Dame E having withdrawals with her two days & overnight in town & no garden trundle – 8.30am lovely long trundle with much oo&ring. ~AUGUST 17, 2000

Michael enjoys holidays in the tropics but finds the plants sometimes monotonous and overblown – he will always prefer a distinct progression of seasons. The diaries diligently follow winter's familiar rhythms, from the last roses of the season to the first 'Winter Cheer' rhododendrons appearing, cycles of beginnings and endings that he and the Boss shared over trundles in rain and wind. Their planting ensured the winter garden always had some flower – camellias and magnolias joining the bulbs and hellebores – but both were happy to see it more restrained than in the heady days of summer, and took special pleasure in arranging winter flowers, their scarcity making them even more precious.

Wonderful snowdrops in the Picking Garden – 40 blooms – do hope the blooms last for Dame E to see. ~JULY 28, 1988

Cut first three daff blooms to include in front hall bowl for Dame E's return tomorrow evening. ~JUNE 8, 1998

Put together a large sheaf of cherry plum blossom – Camellias – Rhodos – Golden Elaeagnus – Eriostemon & Magnolia for Mrs B.'s funeral at 11am this morning – sad to think these are the last flowers I shall be doing for her – over the past years have made a good many posies for Mrs B. ~AUGUST 21, 2001

The garden is at its quietest now, which means time for winter work to be done before the return of spring blossom and visitors – the last of autumn's leaves to collect and mulch, wayward seedlings to evict and vital maintenance work to begin. Michael rakes the last drifts of elm leaves off the round lawn in the fresh-smelling rain, thinking as he does how their golden colour makes it seem, even on grey days, as if the sun is shining.

Productive day spent in the garden with Dame E – morning replaced rotten tea-tree timbers round Old Fashioned Rose garden & opposite border – with new logs from back drive. Afternoon spent in the nursery repotting Liliums. *~JULY 7, 1984*

Temp 13 – Morning employed in Old Fashioned Rose bed collecting diseased leaves – removing unwanted uninvited forget-me-nots foxgloves and other seedlings before forking bed over – what a relief to have this bed behind us – Dame E spent a most productive morning armed with leaf rake removing rubbish from under tea-tree hedge. DE picked lovely mixed bunch of violets. *~AUGUST 3, 1985*

Winter was always the pair's best opportunity to renew and rejuvenate, and they spent the season focused on pruning, transplanting and feeding tired soil. It was the moment to 'have a serious word' with overgrown plants, and deal decisively with those they felt 'weren't earning their keep', the Boss forever urging Michael to be more ruthless.

Began preparing old camellia in Lilium bed to be moved to new position below cottage garage. Dame E and I have longed to move this camellia for the past few years – but could not think where – and did not feel we could just dump this old friend. *~AUGUST 11, 1987*

My morning spent removing several barrow loads of forget-me-nots from Old Fashioned Rose bed – always tempted to leave them as flower – very useful for posies this time of year – but Dame E quite rightly said must be strong-minded – forget-me-not rather too heavy a cover for the bulbs. *~JULY 12, 1999*

Morning employed barrowing compost to Walled Garden which ran out of steam last summer due to not enough nourishment – only a light feed of fowl manure – with double go of fowl and compost hope to strengthen the flowering. *~JULY 16, 2003*

Without the demands of continual watering and deadheading, there's more time for planning and building in the garden, the woodsheds full of neatly stacked firewood and smoke puffing industriously from the chimneys.

OVERLEAF, CLOCKWISE FROM TOP LEFT Japonica, hellebores, *Garrya elliptica* and camellia – there are plenty of treasures in this quietest of seasons.

OVERLEAF, RIGHT The strength of wood against sky – one of Michael's favourite winter sights.

Exciting day spent in the garden with Dame E – much oo&ring –
wonderful weather – looked at redevelopments in evergreen Oak bed
– most enjoyed visit to Oliver's Hill nursery – 4 large pink Azaleas –
exciting addition to native garden yesterday in the form of a wonderful
seat & two tables cut out of the Blue Gum trunk. ~ *JUNE 14, 1984*

Long discussion over breakfast tea pot re new brick pedestal for the
camphor laurel urn. ~ *JUNE 13, 2002*

While the lawns are only being cut once a week, they will soon explode
into spring growth and late winter is the time to treat them to a top
dressing of rich chicken manure, carefully laid and watered in to avoid any
burning of the grass, weather forecasts closely examined to pick the right
moment. It was a ritual both the Dame and Michael loved, the Boss often
commenting how comforting she found the pungent smell.

Remainder of my day employed fertilising all court side & sculpture
lawns – hand hosing in despite constant showers through the day
– always worried about burn of fertiliser dust not well washed in
– Barb thinks I have lost the plot in wet weather gear watering the
lawns in the middle of yet another heavy shower – the Boss explain-
ing to her Michael will be fertilising the Lawns. ~ *AUGUST 11, 2012*

Bulbs are pushing up through the cold ground and, framing the tool room
door, a large *Garrya elliptica* is covered with fragrant velvety catkins. The
late winter blossoms of the cherry plums are lighting up the garden, and
sweet peas, planted in March from the previous year's seed, are slowly
climbing their frames, Dame Elisabeth waiting to see if there were any of
her favourite blues, which she loved giving to friends.

Spent afternoon planting hundreds of English daisies around dam
banks and cottage areas – they will continue the flow in spring.
~ *JUNE 20, 1987*

Planted further 150 English daisy – method – drop plant in puddle
and stomp on it. ~ *JUNE 27, 1987*

Dame E suggests perhaps a good day to get the tray of *Eucalyptus
cypellocarpa* out – on our last trundle the Boss had spent some time

Winter reveals the beauty
of liquidambars adorned
with seed pods, paperwhites
and snowflakes in flower at
their feet.

in farm nursery discussing plant material and where they were to be planted – 3pm 66 young trees planted & watered with tree guards. *~ JUNE 15, 2010*

Michael says they tried for years to convince dubious friends rugged up during long trundles that winter was the best of seasons at Cruden, and even at 101 the Boss was still delighting in it.

4pm – mild, sunny – Dame E dressed for tonight's dinner party decides she cannot miss the moment for a trundle – the Boss in great form. *~ JULY 27, 2010*

By late winter, most of the autumn leaves have been collected for mulching, though the Laughing Tree is just getting started. This giant evergreen oak, *Quercus* 'Firthii', a rare hybrid that in full leaf resembles an enormous waterfall of tumbling green, is only now beginning to drop in earnest. Planted as a sapling by the Dame in the 1930s and given its nickname many years ago for the quip that it must be laughing at those toiling to collect the many thousands of leaves it scatters below, this heritage-listed tree will make work for them until spring.

Very cold early morning white frost – my first two hours employed with leaf rake gathering numerous Firthii leaves – also by far the best way of getting warm. *~ JULY 22, 2002*

7am – Rake up Firthii leaves from Umbrella lawn – tree dropping quite seriously now – though many weeks of cleaning up to go. *~ AUGUST 16, 2005*

One of winter's other chief tasks is tending to Cruden's glorious collection of more than 300 roses in the Picking Garden and the Old Fashioned Rose bed, which have finally finished after many weeks of spectacular flowering.

Never completely bare, Cruden's extraordinary Laughing Tree (*Quercus* 'Firthii') sheds vast numbers of leaves on lawns and beds below, even as it sprouts new ones.

7.30am – fine clear morning. Day spent on hands and knees collecting every last diseased rose leaf before spreading between the four beds 10 lovely bags of sheep manure. Finishing the job by forking the beds over and raking paths before Dame E returns tomorrow. Lovely feeling having roses in such good health. *~ JULY 15, 1986*

Very happy four hours spent with Dame E in the Picking Garden planting the six new roses. ~ *JULY 29, 1991*

Michael has been pruning some of these roses, such as the two thick-branched 'Climbing Peace' bushes transplanted in the 1980s from the original walled rose bed, since his first days in the garden, and still reels off their names and origins with ease. For many years he and the Dame tackled the roses together and Michael still prunes hard, as she did, and misses her eagle eye spotting the places where he'd been lenient. Once the pruning is complete, the beds are 'tickled up' with a garden fork and sprayed with lime sulphur. 'It's a good feeling to know they're well taken care of,' he says.

My day employed removing pushy buttercups from long flat border with a break during heavy shower late morning to see Dame E's wonderful photos of her Irish & France garden tours. Afternoon with Dame E's help went over the pruning of the roses removing some rather bad limbs I had missed. Become blind after pruning for a while – missed Dame E's help this year. ~ *AUGUST 11, 1988*

Begin pruning the Iceberg hedge – hate pruning these roses – they bloom on so bravely right to the very last. ~ *JULY 19, 1992*

Though some of her family insisted that her old timber home felt like a fridge in winter, the Boss always refused to have it centrally heated, firmly believing that too much heat was weakening. Michael too would always rather be outside. It's not surprising then that they were rarely put off by winter's discomforts, Michael liking to rib that only 'townies' are ever bothered by gardening in bad weather.

Fine cold – good morning to warm up on the end of a Shovel. ~ *JULY 13, 1993*

Dame E coming to cheer Ken & I on continuing the clear out of the long border – DE said she was pleased not to have to join us in this bitter weather – However as I pointed out to her she spent many long years in all weathers doing these very same jobs when she had very little help. ~ *JUNE 5, 2000*

Really getting very cold & dark by 4.30pm with the low cloud cover. Dame E & Joe leave for Government House – I feel very grateful that I am going home to a quiet night by the fire – think the Boss quite wonderful – 101 and heading off on an evening out on this cold winter's night. *~ JUNE 8, 2010*

But when the weather was truly awful, they took the garden inside, retreating to go through plant catalogues together and draw up wish-lists, or sort through boxfuls of Dame Elisabeth's garden photos.

Very pleasant four hours spent with Dame E in front of the school-room fire – with three card tables – two part-filled albums and one large new – we set about grading the photos – removing all from part-filled – some very good – some only good for the fire – Having placed the possible photos in groups of area of the garden we then graded as Dame E placed them into albums. Lily came and laid by the fire – giving us support in her company. *~ JUNE 12, 1993*

As the days gradually start growing longer, Michael knows the peaceful time when the garden can catch its breath is coming to an end ahead of the riot of spring, and that the hard work done now in the garden will pay off in the months ahead.

Complete the forking over of Walled Garden beds – very pleased with the condition of the soil – if Walled Garden not a screaming success this summer – think perhaps potatoes. *~ AUGUST 27, 1996*

There's a sense of urgency in these jobs by late winter, for reflected in large puddles on the gravel drive are masses of small brown-pink buds that are spreading through the branches of the giant elms like mist. Slowly but unstoppably, the garden is on the move.

CHAPTER FIVE

The Spring Garden

7am – Dame E waiting with the buggy on my arrival to go for an early oo&r drive in the garden before her busy day gets underway – garden a treat – just every corner bursting with lovely spring growth & bloom – so filled with promise. *~ NOVEMBER 10, 1994*

Spring arrives at Cruden in clouds of elm blossom swirling through the garden like confetti. Their grand winter solemnity suddenly shed, the elms in front of the house are now covered with pom-pom clusters of blossom the colour of Granny Smith apples. Fragrant breezes send the tiny flowers dancing through open windows and doors into the house, where they will be found in days to come hidden behind sofas and under chairs. In a week or two most of the blossom will have faded and fallen, waiting to be raked up and taken away by the barrow load. But for now it is merriment in motion.

Garden really at that special minute in time with so much lovely soft spring flower and the promise of more to come. *~ OCTOBER 17, 1994*

In the corner of Dame Elisabeth's sitting room, catching the sunlight which spills through the window, a large glass vase is filled with long sprays of elm blossom and the graceful green and white goddess lilies now flowering around the lake. It's a simple but spectacular arrangement and a ritual full of meaning, for Michael has been collecting these same flowers

The fluttering apple-green of elm blossom announces the arrival of spring at Cruden.

OVERLEAF The Picking Garden in its dazzling spring dress, one of the garden's four obelisks almost hidden by new growth.

at the beginning of spring for decades. It's his way of welcoming the new season, a time which brings a giddy abundance of choice for his bouquets.

What better place to spend my birthday than in the Walled Garden at Cruden Farm. ~ *SEPTEMBER 12, 1994*

Lovely spring day – early morning oo&r trundle with Dame E collecting bunch of lilac, Doris Downs roses & sweet pea en route for Dame E to take to her lunch hostess – more flower out each day. ~ *OCTOBER 9, 2000*

As a boy, Michael watched his mother fill a vase every Saturday with flowers from her small garden after she had finished baking. She often mixed the few blooms she had with some eucalypt foliage – something her son still does. Arriving at Cruden, Michael discovered that his new boss also loved filling her house with treasures from the garden, and did it with enviable skill. 'She was very good at letting air and light through the flowers, the first person I saw do them so naturally,' he recalls. As always Michael says the Dame taught him everything, but he clearly has his own special flair.

Dame Elisabeth saw that too, and soon invited Michael to help her. 'I think she caught me peering through the window at her arrangements quite often, and she knew how much pleasure it gave me to do them,' he says. He still remembers vividly the moment she asked him, more than twenty years ago, to arrange the Christmas house flowers for the first time; and he has since done hundreds of arrangements for the house and for posies, parties, funerals and weddings, whether they were held in the garden, at Dame Elisabeth's local parish church or further afield, the pair balancing buckets of flowers behind seats and on their laps as they drove them into town.

After the serenity of the winter garden, spring is full not only of growth but of sound, from the many blackbirds chattering as they dart and dig through the beds to the talk of visitors admiring the season. Ducklings skitter in shy groups around the lake and the many nests perched in trees, shrubs and even hidden away in the standard roses are full of the hungry clamour of new life. These lucky fledglings have ringside seats, for the rectangular Picking Garden, with its large beds separated by straight paths widened over time to accommodate the buggy, is bursting with promise; young foxgloves, clematis, fine stems of lavender and catmint are beginning to spill over bed edges. Rose bushes heavy with buds are surrounded by the first poppy flowers, full of frantic bees caked in pollen. Nearby, five standard 'Renae' roses the size of small trees form a joyous border of pink and green, punctuated by glints of the lake beyond.

DE keeps saying I do not want to leave Cruden Farm in its spring dress. *~ SEPTEMBER 7, 1993*

Dame E and I purring with pleasure at the picture the garden makes as we return from Cranhaven Gate – Gate house so much part of the landscape now – Cherry plum in full bloom – *Prunus* 'Elvins' & Malus full of promise. Yellow jasmine back of Long border good colour company for the later bulbs. Silver chimes which seemed barely out of the ground last week begin to bloom – garden a treat. *~ SEPTEMBER 2, 1999*

In the long border, the dark soil is fast vanishing under a green haze as hardy perennials like sedums and phlox sprout skywards. Young delphiniums unfurl in a sea of nodding forget-me-nots and buttercups, the latter spreading so enthusiastically that soon Michael will reluctantly have to pull many out – saving some for a glass jar on the kitchen windowsill. Towering above them the scarlet goblets of *Magnolia liliiflora* 'Nigra' pick up the colour of the mauve echium spires nearby, while white peonies mingle with the flowering broom, its many stems as elegant as dancers' arms, and lime-green euphorbias echo the bright elm blossom. There's loveliness at every turn.

Difficult to get on – so much to enjoy. *~ NOVEMBER 1, 1993*

Another perfect morning – Dame E off to early church via Lake & back drive says she just cannot get enough of the Farm after three days in Town – arriving home with 8 people from church to see the garden. *~ OCTOBER 23, 1994*

Though sorry to farewell winter, Michael can't resist spring's sense of renewal. 'There's a relief in seeing everything looking so healthy,' he says. 'You can see the soft green popping out on everything.' Winter's sharp outlines have been replaced by plump balls of new foliage, and though the trees have lost some of the individuality so accentuated in winter by their

OVERLEAF, LEFT It lasts only a week or two but the bewitching spring exuberance of *Prunus* 'Elvins' is worth the wait.

OVERLEAF, RIGHT Bees crowd the garden's poppies in noisy delight.

bare wood, they've gained a fresh charm as light shimmers through the young canopies. With their return, the open panoramas of winter have closed in again, the garden reclaiming its sense of mystery as the visitor wanders the leafy tunnels.

Visit from Mrs D. Full of admiration for the garden. (Can't imagine why she went to England looking at gardens when Cruden Farm so close). ~ *SEPTEMBER 18, 1985*

Lovely long drive around the Farm and outer garden – on our return Dame E keeps saying it is a very special spring.
~ *SEPTEMBER 24, 2005*

Many of the flowering trees, like the *Prunus* 'Elvins' at the bottom of the cottage garden, are now at their most luminous. For days this flowering plum has been producing thousands of tight buds in cream and pink and then, almost overnight, its lichen-mottled branches vanish under a cascading froth of blossom. For two precious weeks every year it is riveting – and unapologetically ebullient, which is why it was planted in an out-of-the-way spot. The two gardeners knew it as 'a five-minute wonder' but loved it nonetheless. 'Dame Elisabeth used to say it was like the sun popping through on a bleak day,' says Michael.

Malus floribunda and White flowering cherries seem lovelier each day though we have thought them perfect for the past week.
~ *SEPTEMBER 29, 1997*

The lawns, soft and lush after their late winter feed, are speckled with tiny white daisies while bluebells run like brushstrokes of vivid blue through the beds. Everywhere Cruden is at its most charming and old-fashioned, reminiscent of a favourite grandmother's garden, filled with hollyhocks, nigella, roses, crowds of columbines and pale-pink quince blooms. 'Even if people don't remember the names, they remember the plants – it's a senti-mental experience,' says Michael.

Cut wonderful lilacs from large tree at Dame E's kitchen window for two large bowls in big sitting room – how marvellous to be able to cut lilac like this. ~ *OCTOBER 21, 2000*

Summer is lovely but then everyone's garden is colourful in summer
– not everyone has so many old Friends in spring. ~ *FEBRUARY 22, 2007*

Some of these old friends, such as forsythia and lilac, are all the more
treasured for their spring cameos. Despite their quiet habits through the
rest of the year, they're special enough for those few weeks to keep their
place in the garden. And if spring is the time for welcoming back old
friends, it's the time for making new ones too.

Lovely walk with Lily around the Lake during which I discovered
two lovely double daffs which have not flowered before – Dame E
suggests I lift a bulb of each and plant in the cottage garden for
safe keeping. ~ *SEPTEMBER 6, 1993*

With the busy hum of bees a steady soundtrack, the garden's energy in
spring is contagious. By mid-spring, Dame Elisabeth was usually back in
the pool for her daily morning swim, often returning to the house
afterwards with a huge assortment of flowers for vases and friends, before
joining Michael whenever she could in the garden.

Very productive morning spent with Dame E weeding grey & white
border. Lunch. Couldn't contain ourselves another minute – afternoon
spent redeveloping under sitting room windows. ~ *SEPTEMBER 29, 1984*

My morning employed removing the hundreds of common impatience seedlings from the rose beds along Hedge path – Impatience
spit their seed across the path from Hedge bed. ~ *SEPTEMBER 18, 1994*

With new discoveries and blossom every day, if either the Dame or Michael
was away, the other fretted they would miss something special.

So very good to be back after two weeks in PNG – garden a dream
– always lovelier when seeing the farm with fresh eyes. Flat cottage
lawns a mass of English daisy – still a reasonable showing of bulbs in
cottage flat gardens and lake banks – *Malus floribunda* heavy in bud
– Dame E says she put the garden on hold for me. ~ *SEPTEMBER 17, 1988*

floribunda in heavy bud – one sunny day they will be out – do hope
they hold for Dame E's return. ~ *SEPTEMBER 9, 1993*

OVERLEAF, LEFT
Cruden's collection of
eupatorium was grown from
a cutting given to the Boss
by her dressmaker.

OVERLEAF, RIGHT The
first hosta shoots bursting
forth as the garden awakes.

To celebrate the season, every year Dame Elisabeth would host a Melbourne Cup weekend lunch on the lawn above the Picking Garden for one hundred guests, she and Michael filling large urns with the long stems of purple *Buddleia alternifolia*. They would then work together in the garden on Cup Day itself, conscious of keeping up with its rapid growth and the often tumultuous weather, with plenty of activity in both soil and sky.

Usual Cup day shared in the garden with Dame E between Picking Garden and main border – both worked solidly for two hours after lunch removing barrow after barrow loads of leaves from front lawns and main border – trying to make some impression on the debris from last night's winds. *~ NOVEMBER 3, 1987*

My day spent dead-heading roses in Picking Garden – end of the day five full wheel barrows and still not done. *~ NOVEMBER 24, 1997*

With spring growth lawns a little out of control – must begin cutting every 2 days for a few weeks to slow growth rate down and regain control. *~ OCTOBER 10, 1998*

While the spring lawns of the main garden are kept in check, the grasses around the lake and in the outer garden are left alone, except for wide paths mown through their slender, swaying stalks, drawing the eye to the farm fields beyond. For the two gardeners, the contrast between the manicured green of the main garden and the knee-high wildness of the surrounding paddocks was one of spring's true highlights. 'Dame Elisabeth always said she found the sight of the grass in flower moving in the breeze very comforting,' Michael recalls.

Really is the most wonderful season – trees growing like steam – all that wonderful lush fresh green – so far no hot north winds to burn their freshness – the paddock and uncut lake grass going to seed – What a sight when the seed heads move in the wind. *~ NOVEMBER 24, 1992*

The Laughing Tree (*Quercus* 'Firthii') interrupts the dreaminess of the garden's pleasures, its unrelenting dropping of leaves reminding them of work to be done. It won't finish swamping the garden beds and lawns below until late spring – by which time it will be in new leaf again.

The old weeping elm with its spring dusting of fresh green growth.

Breeze strengthening into strong wind mid-afternoon – front border where I spent most of yesterday removing barrow after barrow of Firthii leaves, edging and composting – now looking quite derelict again – so disappointing. ~ *OCTOBER 22, 2002*

Firthii leaves down in bulk – spend next 4 hours raking up numerous barrow loads – though by 10am would think a leaf has not been picked up for weeks. ~ *SEPTEMBER 1, 2013*

Its activity coincides with the return of visitors to the garden, with functions and tours resuming in earnest. Winter's efforts are proving their worth, and Michael is beginning to look after young dahlias, which will bloom right through until the end of autumn, a signature flower at Cruden that needs much of his time and help.

Old Fashioned Rose bed looks a dream with Aquilegia, nigella & foxgloves in full bloom with roses giving a lovely natural look – roses well worth the day of agony Dame E & self went through pruning & tying down. ~ *NOVEMBER 16, 1985*

Breeze dropping slightly – decide to risk spraying Picking Garden paths – So difficult these days to get a time when people are not walking around the garden. ~ *OCTOBER 20, 2002*

Re-staking – tying up of Dahlias Walled Garden & long border – rather difficult to stake & tie dahlias without making them look like a bag of chaff tied to stakes. The Boss believed in regular light tying in so the dahlias kept their figures without stakes being seen too much. ~ *NOVEMBER 24, 2013*

November has traditionally been full of open days, charity events and lunches, and visits from friends and family, with the Dame keeping up her daily whirlwind of appointments and visitors into her late nineties.

Dame E completed the 30 table bowls of flowers yesterday and put them in the cool of dining room – by 11.30am all in place – Tent looks a treat. ~ *OCTOBER 16, 1994*

Spring brings a profusion of flowers and foliage, from the bronze-coloured new leaves of the roses to richly coloured spires of echium and larkspur.

OVERLEAF, LEFT
Sweetly scented mignonette, introduced to Cruden as seed given to the Dame by a country friend many years ago, brings stunning spring texture.

OVERLEAF, RIGHT The endless bounty of spring.

4.30pm Dame E & Joe leave for town – have only seen Dame E in the distance since breakfast – spending the morning at her desk – lunch guests DE took for a trundle in the lovely spring sun – lunch guests no sooner gone than Simon Ambrose from McClelland Gallery here. As Simon leaves Graeme Miller arrives – Graeme leaves just as Joe brings No. 12 to front door – just another quiet day. ~ SEPTEMBER 5, 2005

With summer fast approaching, Michael takes his last holiday before months of heat send the garden into overdrive, and pauses to appreciate spring's freshness. 'When it's all out it can be a little too towny for Cruden, a bit too much,' he says of summer's peak, particularly in the Picking Garden. 'In a smaller garden in town you'd be thrilled because it would add a bit of glamour, but here when it's competing with the park effect of the lake and the trees, it can be a bit too much of a good thing – not quite Cruden.'

The Picking Garden breath-taking with Austin roses on supports in full bloom – remainder of roses about a third out – just about perfect to Dame E & my eye – when all in full bloom feel rather over the top – Dame E busy with 3 separate groups to the garden over the day. ~ NOVEMBER 3, 1998

If there's a downside to spring for Michael, it's that sometimes, surrounded by so much tender young growth, he can't help feeling that the garden suddenly seems almost vulnerable. Though it's easy to feel very far from summer's trials when sitting under a rustling young oak at Cruden in the cool morning light, he's already readying himself for the unpredictable months ahead.

Roses, foxgloves, poppies, Sweet peas, Alstroemeria & Clematis just dreamy almost too lovely – in a strange way almost makes me feel nervous with so many dreadful things happening in the world.
~ NOVEMBER 11, 2002

Preparing means toughening up the spring garden by keeping the watering to just the right level so that it can cope with any sudden onslaught of heat – too much water and it's overly soft, too little and it's parched. By mid-spring, the weekly watering of the garden's fifty freshly composted tubs has begun again after a winter break, along with the more fragile patches of lawn. Adding compost and mulch to garden beds must be finished too, before the hot weather arrives.

> Temp 35 6am began watering – dreadful night and worse to come today – garden too soft to handle heat – myself also – depressing day little else achieved apart from the watering. *~ NOVEMBER 2, 1987*

> So lovely to be working in lovely fresh-smelling rain.
> *~ SEPTEMBER 16, 2002*

Michael will long many times for rain in the coming months, watching the sky and waking in the night hoping to hear the sound of rain on his own roof, because that means it may reach Cruden too. Already the long grasses beyond the lake are turning gold, the spring green ebbing from the fields like the tide. The carefree charms of spring are about to be replaced by a far more testing season.

OVERLEAF Looking across a sea of lawn daisies to the lake and the metal sculpture 'Ibis' on Willow Island.

CHAPTER SIX

The Summer Garden

7am perfect – lovely sunny morning – garden a dream – how very lucky we are to enjoy the loveliest garden surely on Earth – thanks to Dame E's commitment to the ongoing care of Cruden Farm.

~ FEBRUARY 24, 1991

The hypnotic whirring of many sprinklers is the unmissable sound of summer at Cruden, their fine spray so refreshing to walk or trundle through on a sweltering morning, as the Dame and Michael used to love to do. On days like these, the heat feels like a heavy blanket thrown over the farm – the cows very still under the trees, Dame Elisabeth's last dog Bonnie panting drowsily in her kennel and the smell of hay on the dry air. Yet the garden is full of energy and the gardeners must be too, for this is the season of relentless growth and heat that Michael most dreads, when he must be more alert than ever. The lazy summer beach days of his youth seem especially far away now, for summer is never carefree for those with gardens to fret over.

I do not care if we never have a hot summer again – However guess nature knows what it's about – the dahlias certainly enjoy the heat. ~ JANUARY 13, 1997

As the roofs and roads of the suburbs shimmer around it in the heat, the garden feels more of a refuge than ever, full of cool nooks and quiet

The burnished gold of the outer paddocks in summer.

OVERLEAF Dame Elisabeth loved to glimpse Cruden's cows wandering beyond the garden.

shaded paths. The deciduous trees again prove their worth, with their dense canopies now throwing generous umbrellas of shade, their green lushness so restful to the sun-dazzled eye. The lake and dams are more important than ever too, for the life-giving water they provide the garden, of course, but also simply for the shimmering glimpses on offer from the many wooden benches set at vantage points around the garden.

Michael and the Dame carefully placed each of these benches, deciding which should be white to catch the eye from afar, and which should be in natural wood to blend with surrounding trunks. One of these is almost hidden under the two vast oaks planted close together by the Dame near the barn in the 1930s, their limbs now mingled in an arboreal embrace beside the lake. She loved to linger underneath and look up through the endless layers of leaves, their veins picked out against the bright light, and in her last years, Michael would drive her under the branches in her car. 'I'm sure you can make it through there,' was her usual encouragement as he inched the old car between garden beds and bushes.

These glorious oaks, now some 30 metres tall, are thought to be hybrids of Algerian oak (*Quercus canariensis)* and the two gardeners fondly referred to them as 'rats' for their uncertain origins. At last count twenty-nine of their offspring have been planted around the farm, though none have yet surpassed their parents in stature. A haunt of visiting blackbirds and children, no one drives under the blended canopies any more and their vast branches have been let grow long enough to sweep the ground like a hooped skirt. It's a perfect bolthole on a hot afternoon, resting on the bench in the dappled light and counting the small acorns growing above.

PREVIOUS PAGE
Freshly watered hostas
contrast with the dry golden
grasses alongside paddock
walking trails.

OPPOSITE The two
gardeners added wooden
benches to the garden
gradually, carefully choosing
the right position for each,
such as this place of
contemplation under an oak.

OVERLEAF The canopies
of Cruden's trees offer
true sanctuary from
summer's heat.

Garden really is in dream time if we can hold it. ~ *JANUARY 12, 1997*

Perhaps leaving the shade for a while, you might walk across to the house, crossing as you do the lawn beyond the Picking Garden. To walk barefoot across a Cruden lawn in summer is a heady experience, the grass soft and springy underfoot, and deliciously cool. At this time of year Michael cuts the main garden lawns higher than normal to protect their roots as much as he can, and hovers over them like an anxious parent. One of his most worrisome 'trouble spots' is the round lawn at the top of the front drive, lying like a pool amid the dust from the gravel drive and such a crucial counterpoint to the pale grass of the parched paddocks, but home to three large thirsty trees. Whenever the Dame questioned the amount of watering

the lawns demanded, Michael reminded her of the garden's subterranean network of tree roots. 'I pointed out that we were watering them just as much as the lawns,' he says. 'That convinced her.'

> Garden always looks cooler when lawns in good order.
> ~ *DECEMBER 11, 1993*

> Afternoon employed in company of Lawn mower – cut all court side Lawns – garden holding up well in the heat – how fortunate we are the Boss had the foresight to put in such good dams.
> ~ *FEBRUARY 23, 2013*

Each spring he delays the start of regular watering for as long as possible to harden the garden like an athlete before a marathon. But once summer descends he is there every morning, often by 5 a.m., watching sunlight streak the stables' spire with gold as he starts the dam pump to feed the hoses. He moves the long-legged metal sprinklers between lawns on small wooden rollers attached to their feet – an ingenious feature added when the Dame had them built by a local hardware store before Michael began at Cruden. Half of those original sprinklers are still in use; the remainder are clever copies made by farm manager Andrew Gobel. In years past Michael would often arrive to find the Dame had begun around 4 a.m., the pair then carting water down to the young trees around the lake in buckets or bins on the buggy, a longing for rain always on their mind.

> 37 forecast for tomorrow – Dame E kept hoses going until late last night – garden holding so far. ~ *JANUARY 18, 1997*

> Wonderful, wonderful rain – First job of the morning after measuring rain and celebrating with Dame E over her breakfast teapot – collect flower material & freshen up house flowers for Dame E's lunch guests. ~ *JANUARY 13, 1998*

The birdlife is grateful too, parrots and kookaburras among the many birds gliding down to the water. Some ducks prefer the quieter setting of the small pool built in the old walled rose bed, joined on many long-ago mornings by Dame Elisabeth or Michael who took turns going for a plunge in between dragging hoses and preparing breakfast.

Summer is a time of constant vigilance for Michael and his fellow gardeners.

Dame E coming up from pool and ready for trundle by 7.15am
– Garden a dream really enough to make a cat purr as old Jack
would say. ~ *JANUARY 16, 1999*

5 am – On with the watering – Kookaburras & Magpies Lovely
early morning – though rather disappointed in the Kookaburras
– am sure I remember my grandfather telling me when the
Kookaburras laughed it meant rain – think ours need retraining
– most mornings they begin at 5.30am as I have my swim having
started the sprinklers – perhaps it's my poor stroke they are
laughing at. ~ *FEBRUARY 15, 2003*

In return for the tireless care given to it, the summer garden repays the
gardeners handsomely with the perfume and colour of many old friends –
nicotiana, Shasta daisies, pink phlox, spikes of dark delphinium, heliotrope,
drifts of salvias and glowing penstemons. Tubs burst with huge-leafed pink,
white and blue hydrangeas and clouds of butterflies mill around the
buddleias. Dahlias in shades of cream, yellow and pink pop with colour,
their proud stems matched by the flowering spears of agapanthus, a striking
and dependable performer that Michael enjoys all the more for it being
unfashionable.

Dame E has enjoyed the most wonderful success with the delphinium seed given to her by Mrs B. – 79 plants in all planted into
various beds of the Walled Garden and Picking Garden – tallest
spike measure 8 Ft. ~ *DECEMBER 31, 1986*

Schoolroom wisteria producing wonderful summer flowering
– lovely perfume through gardens – counted 200 blooms which
I think rather good for a summer flowering. ~ *DECEMBER 21, 1987*

Garden groaning with blooms – particularly the Picking Garden
– Roses heavy in bloom – first Dahlias – Glads & sweet peas
– Alstroemeria – perennial Gyp – in fact an embarrassment –
but don't we love it. ~ *DECEMBER 20, 1992*

Such boisterousness requires days of non-stop deadheading, a job that
must be kept up with, both to encourage more blooms and to ensure the
garden looks its best for summer guests. When the roses are at their peak,

Buddleia attract clouds
of butterflies.

Michael fills barrow after barrow with their faded beauty, though he delays deadheading in very high temperatures, hoping the spent heads will provide any new buds with some shelter from the sun.

> Morning spent in Walled Garden trimming Anthemis which has gone quite mad with rain & warmth – threatens to spread across grass walk. ~ *DECEMBER 11, 1985*

> The Ken Myers here – Mr M armed with his pruners – deadheading as they walk round the garden – must think Dame E and I have been slacking off. ~ *JANUARY 11, 1986*

> Lovely mid-morning trundle with Dame E which turned into a very productive 1½ hours of deadheading. ~ *JANUARY 17, 2002*

After their early season feed and compost, Cruden's roses are the star of the summer garden, and none more so than the 'Dame Elisabeth Murdoch' roses – the sweetly scented hybrid tea created in honour of the Dame in 2002. Flushed with the peach and yellow tones of a summer sunrise, it's healthy and vigorous even in the fiercest conditions, and thrives in Cruden's soil. 'Tough as old boots, just like me,' pronounced Dame Elisabeth when Michael mentioned how well they were flourishing.

> Most of my day spent watering – impossible to keep enough water on with such a hot north wind – leave hose soaking under Hydrangea all day – despite having Picking Garden well-watered before main heat of the day blooms just burning up before my eyes – very depressing – the only Roses not to seem affected are the bed of Dame Elisabeth Murdoch roses – even the foliage lovely & fresh healthy green with some young bronze shoots. ~ *FEBRUARY 3, 2001*

> Lovely early trundle – Walled Garden a picture, so much stronger – more colour than last January. Dame Elisabeth Murdoch roses heavy in bud again after what seems only a week's rest.
> ~ *JANUARY 3, 2003*

The 'Dame Elisabeth Murdoch' rose is tough and generous, much like the woman it was named for.

OVERLEAF Chief among summer's parade of blooms are Cruden's collection of more than 300 roses (125 varieties), including the climbing tea 'Devoniensis' (left).

Roses feature frequently in Michael's summer bouquets for the house, and in the many Christmas posies he made for Dame Elisabeth to deliver. December was typically one of her – and Cruden's – busiest times,

her letterbox filling with forty or more Christmas cards a day, each of which she replied to with her own handwritten cards. There was always also a flurry of events, speeches, parties and dinners and the annual Cruden community carols' night in one of the paddocks.

> Cut five posies for Dame E to deliver to various friends (great fun).
> ~ *DECEMBER 13, 1988*

> 7am – day employed with Dame E deadheading and thinning out Walled Garden and Picking Garden – some mowing in the afternoon. ~ *CHRISTMAS EVE, 1988*

> Garden a dream – Lilium along central steps & folly path of Picking Garden magnificent – almost indecent – a good six feet tall with numerous bells – sweet peas still blooming with Dame Elisabeth cutting lovely bunches – catch up on Christmas news with Dame E over breakfast. ~ *DECEMBER 27, 1987*

As summer marches on into the New Year, seed from the garden is dry enough to be harvested, Michael shaking the double poppy heads to scatter their contents through the Picking Garden before rats raid the seed pods. He and his fellow gardeners summer prune the vines, roses and espaliered floribundas, and remove the agapanthus seed heads before taking out the orange blooms of the day lilies and canna lilies that the Dame thought too florid, leaving only their rich purple foliage to add depth to the perennial borders.

> Cheered on by Dame E made war on the now very over poppies removing all except for the few marked ones (good doubles) to be kept for seed – much too wet to be collected – at the end of the day the Picking Garden looked so much cleaner and fresher – the over material distracts so much from the good. ~ *DECEMBER 30, 1993*

> Collect seed & remove the over Larkspur and sweet peas – forking over beds – Looks so much better – nothing takes more out of the overall picture than over plant material. ~ *FEBRUARY 10, 1996*

In the Picking Garden vegetables mingle with the flowers, corn stalks shooting up like saplings next to aromatic basil and tomato bushes. Though he likes the garden's garlic flowers and dill as decorative plants, Michael confesses to taking little interest in Cruden's edible plants – after all, they're no use at all for vases. Nearby, across a field of rippling golden grasses, the trio of gnarled old pear trees, the only remnants of the original farm orchard, are laden with a ripening crop of pears, their smooth skin burnished purple. They have been fruiting at year's end for many decades, and in the diaries Michael contemplates the year just gone, and those yet to come.

> Another very happy exciting and productive year in the garden at Cruden Farm. How lucky we all are. ~ *DECEMBER 31, 1991*

> Another wonderful year shared in the garden with Dame E. ~ *DECEMBER 31, 2002*

After frantic December, the silver lining of summer was always January, when the holiday season meant Dame Elisabeth was, for a few weeks, free of many of her philanthropic commitments and at home in the garden more than at any other time of the year.

> 7am – My day spent giving lilium & iris bed a good going over while Dame E on the other side of the wall gave the Walled Garden a fright, removing barrow loads of over material and took the pushy Anthemis to task which since its last trim not content with spreading over the grass had decided to take over phlox and delphiniums as well. ~ *JANUARY 25, 1986*

> Dame E cut armfuls of wonderful Glads and then set out to deliver them to various grateful friends. ~ *JANUARY 17, 1987*

She and her No. 2 Gardener spent these weeks keeping the garden ready for visitors, welcoming garden tours, friends and sightseers arriving in convoys of cars or coaches, setting up chairs in the shade beside the lake, inviting people to picnic under the trees and overseeing the erection of giant marquees for spectacular parties.

> Added excitement for the men – Dolly Parton among the guests. Dame E cutting roses by the armful for the house and giveaways. Dahlias improving at last – weather has been too mild for them

OVERLEAF The sculptural elegance of papyrus around the lake, and slender stalks of chive flowers in the Picking Garden (right).

127

– do not think they will make their height in Walled Garden which rather spoils the scale. *~FEBRUARY 7, 1987*

Make a start on the 12 table bowls for tent – rather nervous with so much lovely material – hate to muck them up. *~ FEBRUARY 7, 2007*

The Dame's February 8 birthday was almost always marked with a celebration in the garden, and Michael spent weeks ensuring that the lawns and flowers would be at their most splendid for those events, heatwaves or not. Though the parties were memorable – 500 guests in a marquee when she turned ninety, 550 when she reached one hundred – the day of her birthday usually began quietly over breakfast with Michael, before playing bridge with friends while the phone rang constantly with birthday wishes.

Dame E's 79th birthday – early morning employed giving drive & paths polish and tickle before guides of Melbourne Botanic Gardens arrive for their walk in the garden and picnic lunch – due to the uncertain weather Dame E has turned the big sitting room over to the guides to lunch in – the guides were quite overwhelmed by her kindness knowing that DE was expecting lunch guests of her own. *~ FEBRUARY 8, 1988*

Garden a dream – Dame E's 91st birthday – down early, no lay in with long day planned – leaving 8.30am to drive herself to town taking two posies to deliver on the way before arriving at the Club 11.30am for the first of her day's celebrations. *~ FEBRUARY 8, 2000*

Disappointing that the lovely standard honeysuckles which were well into their second blooming for DE's birthday last year are barely showing a bud today. *~ FEBRUARY 8, 2004*

For her birthday Michael often gave the Dame plants – perhaps a hydrangea or some kangaroo paw, and one year a climbing rose named for Edna Walling, the formidable designer who reportedly had little time for the ideas of the young bride she met at Cruden Farm. 'Thank you, Michael,' the Dame said with a mischievous smile when she saw that gift. 'Though you know I didn't care much for the woman herself.' The rose was planted nonetheless, if not quite centre stage, and still thrives on the side of the woodshed from where it provides wonderful creamy blooms for the house.

At the height of summer Dame Elisabeth kept her home's heavy curtains drawn, but on especially hot days, even its normally cool rooms are stuffy. Outside Michael quickly rakes up the debris of bark and branches when the wind's up, always anxious about the risk of a grass fire threatening the trees or the timber house. At times he covers hostas and other sensitive plants with umbrellas and shade cloth and finds a shady spot to weed in, or goes home, returning at sundown to keep working. On the most scorching of days, he might even reluctantly succumb to wearing an old straw hat.

I think the first time in years I have not put fresh flowers in when Dame E away for her return – but today even early morning flowers wilting. ~ NOVEMBER 30, 2003

For though summer is exhilarating, it's exhausting too, and the gardeners themselves often wonder if they will wilt as well. As Michael watches the garden and weather forecasts like a hawk, he also looks for that first suggestion of a different colour in a leaf here or there, for the arrival of a certain, barely discernible change in the light over the lake – for the first welcome reminder that even summer's great hurrah must come to an end.

Widening of back drive through bush hill opposite the shack completed – such an improvement – cannot wait to plant in again – must be patient until autumn. ~ FEBRUARY 13, 2012

CHAPTER SEVEN

The Autumn Garden

Walled and Picking Gardens so lovely soft & blousey – as Dame E remarked yesterday rather like a bowl of perfect full blown roses just before they begin to fall. ~ *MARCH 20, 1994*

After the intensity of summer, autumn descends on Cruden like an exhalation of relief. The dazzling cerulean skies are disappearing and the garden is filling with the new season's languid light. The garden beds are fading too, and though there is still much in flower, the garden is taking on the 'blousey' look of muted loveliness that Dame Elisabeth and Michael preferred to the glamour of summer. Both the garden and gardeners are ready for rest, after the long days of summer watering and deadheading, the hectic social calendar and the anxious watching of the weather.

Garden really is a dream this time of year with its earliest hint of Autumn colour – the Summer blooms continue but rather less intense at this time – much softer – some areas just a hint of what has been to lead you on to the next area. ~ *MARCH 20, 2000*

The first hints of autumn spread like a rumour across the garden, glimpsed at the very tops of canopies and around leaf edges. Among the first trees to turn are the two Manchurian pears, *Pyrus ussuriensis*, at the far end of the lake, their rounded canopies now glinting orange and red.

Autumn's flush of colour in one of Cruden's many pin oaks.

OVERLEAF The fiery tones of a weeping *Nyssa sylvatica* on the lake's edge, planted by Dame Elisabeth's granddaughter Penny Fowler, with the house in the background.

They're followed in flaming golds and russets by the oak, maple, nyssa and liquidambar trees across the garden glowing like giant lanterns, as if lit from within.

> Lovely hour off 11am to accompany Dame E on oo&r buggy drive of garden lake area & barn paddock – while there marking positions for the three Delatite oaks to be planted – much oo&ring over the Farm's lovely autumn colours – how lucky we all are to enjoy this lovely patch of ground. ~ *APRIL 20, 1996*

The diaries record many happy trundles at this time of year, both gardeners relishing the way the stonework of the stables, chimneys and garden walls were complemented by autumn's tones. They delighted in the growth of the younger trees around the lake for it meant, says Michael, 'there was more autumn each year', the glad colours reminding them of the old tapestries and open fires they both loved.

> 11.30am – As Dame E leaves she stops by to cheer me on and say how lovely the posies are – Looking at her watch says she has just enough time for a drive round the lake, would I join her – cannot bear to leave without enjoying the Autumn colour of the outer garden. ~ *MAY 31, 2005*

When he stands under the claret-coloured canopy of the maple behind the house, Michael thinks of Lily, Dame Elisabeth's beloved German Shepherd, who died in 1995 and is buried at its feet under masses of violets. When she wasn't keeping the pair company as they worked in the garden, or lying on the grass under the Dame's bedroom window, Lily would join Michael on dawn walks among the pin oaks, which in autumn resemble a row of gleaming bronze pyramids around the lake.

> Miss Lily's welcome this morning – but somehow feel her about the garden – think she will always be here. ~ *MARCH 9, 1995*

Near Lily's resting spot, the garden bed at the feet of the Laughing Tree is carpeted with the white blooms of the groundcover plectranthus, which was always one of the two gardeners' autumn favourites, full of both memory and colour.

The play between Cruden's autumnal foliage and the caramel tones of the stables' stonework on show.

OVERLEAF The white blooms of the groundcover plectranthus catching the mellow light under the Laughing Tree.

Very strong yet soft mauve purple giving much warmth at this time
– also brings Lady Bolte to Dame E's thoughts as it was she who
gave Dame E this Plectranthus. ~ APRIL 25, 1996

Easter would herald an end to the Dame's early-morning swims in the
unheated pool, which she had begun in early spring. One Easter brought
3000 visitors to the garden for a charity Easter egg hunt – hundreds of
children fossicked through the garden, some offering to share their finds
with Dame Elisabeth as she watched delightedly from the buggy. She and
Michael spent many Easter weekends together in the garden, and he still
spends the holiday there, often thinking of those times.

7am – breakfast Dame E reports pool a little cold but very refresh-
ing – Lovely mid-morning trundle with Dame E – very pleased with
Old Fashioned bed cannot wait to plant new Roses. ~ APRIL 10, 2007

Plant winter bulbs in groups along grass walk from Gate into barn
paddock to Leylandii hill – Cruden very quiet – miss the Boss.
~ APRIL 20, 2014

It's the season for collecting baskets of walnuts, of the copper beech
drowning the garden around it in showers of its spiky egg-shaped seed
pods, of the first yellow crocus peering out from under the passionfruit
vine and the bold garnish of scarlet hips on the rambling rugosa roses. The
perfume of the lemon spires of the mahonias swirls through the garden,
mixing with the mouth-watering aroma of furry, ripe quinces.

One year Michael counts fifty stems of white belladonna lilies as he
picks for his favourite arrangement of autumn flowers for the house –
green hydrangeas, bunches of red hawthorn berries and bright pin oak
leaves. They light up the house, lasting for days in the cool rooms.
As a younger man Michael used to climb onto the roof to cut branches of
majestic beech foliage for vases throughout the house, their effect as
captivating as the paintings around them.

Garden looking lovely in the fading autumn light – the orange golds
of the birches, oaks & cherries somehow seem even denser in colour
– reflections in the lake so crystal clear – with water level so low the
stone bridge reflection a full circle. ~ MAY 13, 1997

After summer's hubris,
autumn brings an ethereal
quality to Cruden.

OVERLEAF, LEFT One of
Michael's autumnal arrangements, featuring hydrangeas,
gladioli, hollyhocks and the
Dame's namesake roses.

OVERLEAF, RIGHT
Glowing hawthorn berries
are symbolic of autumn, and
one of Michael's constant
choices for autumn posies.

As much as they wanted to linger among such beauty, as always there was much for the gardeners to do, with plenty of deadheading and weeding needed to keep the garden going for the last few functions before its winter hiatus.

> Dame E hard at work removing pushy violets and nut grass from Iceberg hedge in Picking Garden. My afternoon employed completing the spreading of straw mulch over bulbs with time off to enjoy a picnic afternoon tea with Dame E on the peninsula – so lovely watching the ducks at play – Dame E had a 10-minute catnap in the sun (unusual to see her still for this length of time) before going off in her cart to collect the hose from the garden to water the bulbs. *~ APRIL 11, 1988*

> Love these foggy mornings – the garden changes its personality it seems almost every few minutes with changing light as the sun comes up through the fog. *~ APRIL 23, 2007*

As a child, Michael thought the orange and lime spikes of kniphofia, or red hot poker flowers, in his grandmother's garden were far too bright and garish. Now, set against the stone walls and illuminated by the autumn sun, he can't imagine the garden without them.

> Kniphofia in Iris bed giving great deal of pleasure with 65 lovely strong spikes showing colour against autumn foliage of Liliums and brown of stone walls. *~ APRIL 26, 1986*

Like the kniphofia, viburnum, phlox and wind anemones are still flourishing, but the dahlias are now the garden's star performer, their eye-catching form and colours carrying the beds. With their statuesque height they need plenty of care to stop them breaking and staking them at the right time is always a challenge, says Michael. 'The Boss didn't like the Walled Garden or the Picking Garden done too early and looking like Stakesville but if you don't stake them early enough they can get away from you.'

Each year Michael works hard to hide the stakes as the plants reach dramatic heights. Some along the back wall of the Walled Garden regularly grew almost 3 metres high, and Michael remembers a few so big that he and the Boss used to clamber onto a small stepladder to deadhead and thin them out. Still, he maintains, 'They're not a lot of work for what they give you.'

Cruden is famous for its dahlias, which bring so much height and eye-catching colour to the garden in autumn.

Onto the deadheading of the Picking Garden – rather lovely with
Roses dahlias phlox & pastel zinnia in bloom… re-stake white
dahlias in front border – white dahlias now a good six foot – also
dark mauve pink in long border a few a good seven foot – worried
they would collapse with heavy rain. *~ MARCH 1, 1997*

Wind is the dahlias' enemy, and the weather Michael likes least – depressing, he says, for both the garden and the gardeners. In autumn it can cause havoc, tossing the treetops and covering the lawns with debris as it sends the treasured leaves to the ground in thick showers. Dame Elisabeth would sometimes arrive home from town with a storm on her heels, calling Michael to help her tie in the borders before the winds arrived.

6am – Decide I cannot wait another minute before going out to
the Farm to check on the garden – am sure after hours of this awful
wind there will not be a dahlia standing – though still quite black
once my eyes become used to it able to see at least most dahlias
standing if in some odd spread shapes – two in long border have
broken their stakes. *~ MARCH 20, 2003*

Afternoon spent mowing back lawns – what a difference – has an
unloved look very quickly this time of year with rotting leaves
& twigs everywhere – so much wind last few days. *~ MAY 30, 1985*

Not ideal weather for Dame E to be on the road – put good log
on schoolroom fire before I leave in the hope Dame E will be
in shortly. *~ MARCH 1, 2003*

Even with the taste of winter in the air, in autumn the gardeners still hope for rain. The garden, weary after summer, flags easily at this time of year and, even if the winds spare them, the autumn leaves drop too early if there's not enough rain. The dams need replenishing after the dry months, and underground the many hundreds of winter bulbs across the outer garden wait for water too.

Wonderful, wonderful rain garden lovely and fresh autumn
leaves should hold to colour now – marvellous for the bulbs.
8am breakfast with Dame E – both feel quite light with relief
after the rain. *~ APRIL 24, 2004*

6am – Water – garden drying out very quickly as is usual in
Autumn – the perennials tired – takes quite a lot of attention
to keep them going for the last few open days. *~ MARCH 27, 2006*

Michael doesn't want to water too much or too often in autumn, preferring
to let the garden dry out before winter, but he knows from long experience
that it's easy to be lulled into complacency by the cooler nights and pay the
price in lost plants and lawn.

As with the soft spring garden going into hot early summer
– always those difficult first weeks when you cannot afford to
take your eyes off for a minute. *~ MARCH 15, 1999*

It was also the time of year Michael and Dame Elisabeth liked to rummage
through the seed basket, looking for their harvest from last year's sweet pea
crop to plant into a bed of fowl manure on St Patrick's Day. If the bush rats
and birds left them any, the Dame would pick 'Beurré Bosc' pears, baking
them with a little lemon rind and cinnamon, sending a bowl home with
Michael for his supper. Together they studied rose and perennials catalogues over afternoon tea by the schoolroom fire, thoughts turning to new
plantings. Vita Sackville-West could have been thinking of them when she
wrote almost a century ago that 'the most noteworthy thing about gardeners
is that they are always optimistic, always enterprising, and never satisfied.
They always look forward to doing something better'.

Lovely morning drive to Wandin through the hills – trees in their
beautiful Autumn leaves – to choose Mt Fuji for cottage garden
– what a treat – missed having Dame E's company – keeping a low
profile this week since hurting her leg on Sat during a slight alterca-
tion with the kitchen steps while replacing light globes. *~ MAY 2, 1985*

Late afternoon trundle with Dame E very pleased with strong
coloured border especially cannas, sedum, white phlox & Dahlias
continue to give lovely soft bloom in white border – always looking to
improve Dame E suggests adding three clumps of Echinacea creamy
white green centre for change of texture next year. *~ MARCH 8, 2003*

Other seeds are ready for planting too – foxgloves and delphiniums – and
perhaps some extra lilium bulbs as well. When the delphinium seedlings

appear, they'll be transplanted into pots and spend the winter sheltered in the nursery, waiting for spring's warmth before they return to the garden.

DE coming to cheer me on before leaving for the day – discovered much to our delight a good many young delphinium Requinii seedlings pushing through around the parent plants – have been worried about getting the seed up – at once lifted 12 of the strongest, potting them on into thumb pots in a good potting mix.
~ *MARCH 17, 1992*

Planted 275 Ranunculus and 50 White Anemones in Picking Garden. ~ *APRIL 17, 1995*

Then suddenly the leaves start falling, the previous year's growth slipping from the trees like a coat being shrugged off. Surely 'leaf litter' is far too bland a description for the sight of so many leaves coating the lawns and paths in sunlit flecks of gold, crimson and copper.

I hear many so-called keen gardeners moaning about the work of autumn leaves – find this attitude difficult to understand – love every minute of autumn – the wonderful warm colours of leaves easing us into the cold damp of winter – such a pleasant sound walking through the fallen leaves. ~ *MAY 23, 1993*

Lovely mild still early morning – garden in dreamtime – lovely autumn leaves quietly falling from the trees – a very calming special time. ~ *MAY 17, 2012*

Raking quickly becomes an enormous job, and on windy days leaves fall as quickly as Michael can rake them up. Though they're lovely underfoot, the sodden leaves threaten to smother the lawns and Michael reluctantly removes them by the trailer load, enjoying the thought that they'll return to the garden as a thick winter mulch.

Hate raking up the leaves – their autumn colour looks so lovely – but cannot allow them to be too thick on the grass. ~ *MAY 2, 1998*

Cold & wet but who cares – day employed raking & collecting leaves. ~ *MAY 18, 2004*

Lawns strewn with fallen leaves bring great beauty and endless raking.

151

Just as the trees are preparing for winter, so must the gardeners. Garden frames and the many dahlia stakes are cleaned and stored. The nursery is tidied and its residents either planted out or given away – Michael admits he is usually the main offender when it comes to keeping plants 'just in case' space can be found. The last of the autumn planting continues in the outer garden, where new drifts of winter bulbs are buried like treasure.

Yesterday afternoon and evening's rain a great relief – perfect morning to plant the bulbs – add 586 mixed daffs to bulb area on peninsula – all planted by lunch time but too windy to cover with straw mulching – as fast as I forked straw on – wind blew it into the lake. ~ *APRIL 9, 1988*

7.30am breakfast – Dame E suggests time has come for Ken and I to attack farm nursery – my saying to visitors we are mainly growing pots of native grasses doesn't quite cut it – be ruthless says Dame E. ~ *APRIL 18, 2006*

The garden hoses that have been so essential in summer are laid out to soften in the late autumn sun so they can be coiled and put away until spring. Winter jobs in the garden are prioritised and holidays planned. Late autumn is the time to cut down the spent beds, a rewarding job that Michael itches to begin and one that must be underway before too many plants drop their seeds, ensuring crowds of uninvited seedlings in spring.

The time has come to begin the cutting down – in one way sad – another a relief. ~ *MAY 24, 1984*

Been cutting down the Walled Garden – what a lovely feeling – the time just comes when you can't stand the grot another minute. ~ *MAY 25, 1992*

Continue the cutting down of the Picking Garden – rubbish trailer full overflowing – difficult to throw debris up so high. ~ *MAY 12, 2002*

In the autumn light, looking through the garden gates towards the outer paddocks, Cruden seems in a world of its own.

OVERLEAF The Walled Garden at its 'blousey' autumn best – as the Dame used to say, like a bowl of roses, their petals about to fall.

The Dame's namesake roses, as robust as ever, are one of the few flowers left now and Michael longs for the look of freshly turned winter soil, of beds covered with a rich blanket of compost and mulch. He gives all the lawns one last feed to take them through winter and then, so quickly he sometimes can't believe it, another cycle of seasons in the garden has passed.

CHAPTER EIGHT

Lawns and Paths

All lawns cut & garden a dream – not a leaf or blade of grass out of place. ~ *OCTOBER 26, 2002*

Michael has often been described as stubborn – a description you suspect he quite enjoys – and perhaps never more so than when it comes to Cruden's lawns, which he attends to with the zeal you'd expect from a perfectionist who worked as a young man on golf courses. His years of tireless care have clearly been worth it, for the six lawns of the main garden are immaculate expanses of emerald green that give the garden much of its tremendous sense of space and calm, anchoring the various tones of sky, leaf and petal, and contrasting with the wilder paddocks and bush beyond.

Lovely sunny morning – quick tickle & polish – makes such a difference to the garden when paths and drive are freshly raked – somehow brings the gravel to life – like well cared for lawns – the lawns and paths a stage for the plants and trees of the garden. ~ *DECEMBER 17, 1989*

Lovely late morning trundle with Dame E – some very productive deadheading en route. Though worried to see outer garden & farm so dry we both love the contrast between the green of the inner garden and straw colour of the dry grass lake mound with the long grass going to seed – really very attractive. ~ *FEBRUARY 2, 2003*

A soft sweep of lawn skirting the Old Fashioned Rose bed towards a welcoming bench.

OVERLEAF As he has for decades, Michael takes great pride in the immaculate state of the front drive.

157

As well as plenty of work, water and skill, a thick skin is useful when keeping lawns like these, for as the two gardeners discovered over the years, some people think lush grass has no place on a water-poor continent, whether watered by a dam or not. Michael and the Dame always responded to their critics by focusing on the joy the lawns clearly bring. 'We'd have mothers kicking off their shoes at open days and saying their children had never walked on real grass,' says Michael. 'One of the things people love most about Cruden is the calmness which comes from the lawns.'

A Kentucky turf mix of bent, fescue and rye grasses, the main lawns were sown as seed by the Dame and Michael in his early years at Cruden. Since then, other types – native dichondras and fine couches – have been allowed to creep into the mix, but the dominant varieties remain those original grasses with their warm yellow undertones that Michael loves for their lively, fresh look, marrying so well with the garden's colour schemes.

His own assessment of the care they're given is brief: 'They're not bowling-green lawns, they are just well cut and well fed.' But anyone who has struggled to keep even a patch of lawn healthy year-round can appreciate the effort required. For a start, unlike most plants, lawns demand attention in every season. They're mown two or three times a week all year except winter, and for many years Michael fed them every six weeks with his own concoction of sulphate of ammonia and sulphate of potash.

Remainder of day spent in company of catcher mowers – cut all main lawns – trim edges of main Grey & White & strong coloured borders – leaving 6.20pm before Dame E arrives home from town to say – Michael you're here much too late – you must go home. ~ *MARCH 24, 1997*

Take a break from holidays to give Lawns & paths a tickle up for the Prahran garden club's visit today – Rain forecast but lovely still morning to rake up. ~ *SEPTEMBER 25, 1999*

Winter is the time for treating moss attacks and picking the right moment when they're dry enough for their weekly mow, Michael often raking the grass first to remove as much moisture as he can. Some areas, like the round lawn in front of the house, need water even in the dead of winter. Many years ago, when two of Dame Elisabeth's grandsons built billycarts as roguish small boys and raced them on ramps set up on this precious grass, they chose their moment carefully too. 'You can bet your sweet life they did it when Granny was out,' laughs Michael.

TOP Looking across a rich carpet of green towards the Front Border and the house.

BOTTOM Michael enjoys the patterning of leaves against the clean lines of hedge and bench – but not for too long.

Temp 13 – Ground very wet – perfect to spread sulphate of iron on moss in back, umbrella & round lawns – use two large bags – not enough – need two more. ~ *JULY 30, 1987*

Year round, leaves must be kept off the lawns to allow rain and light through – in autumn and early winter this is an endless task. Late winter is the time each year for aerating the lawns and top-dressing them with dry chicken manure to strengthen them ahead of prolonged hot spells and the foot traffic of thousands of spring and summer visitors. It's a job Michael and his fellow gardeners undertake with meticulous care.

More rain during the night – makes feeding back lawns a little more difficult if not careful – fertiliser dust sticks to wet grass and burns – must be careful to wash in well – which creates good deal of comment when seen hand-watering after all this rain. ~ *NOVEMBER 9, 1993*

Most unpleasant gusty winds – not a very pleasant day for spreading fowl manure – in one way wind makes spreading of manure easy but rather spreads manure too far afield after covering me in the dry dust. Not so good for the sinus. ~ *SEPTEMBER 3, 1998*

Spring brings rapid growth that must be reined in, and summer means constant watering and watching for trouble. After so many years caring for the same lawns, Michael can tell with one glance whether an area is hungry or thirsty – or will be tomorrow. 'You can't ever get slack about keeping your eyes on these sort of things,' he says.

Just holding lawns at present – any trouble spot missed for a day is gone the next. ~ *JANUARY 1, 1997*

5am – Light rain early hours of this morning though not enough to clear the air – very warm humid & unpleasant – all I can think of is great weather for fungus. ~ *FEBRUARY 25, 2006*

TOP This stretch of lawn is often trampled by crowds on open days and needs careful maintenance.

BOTTOM Thoughtfully-placed benches offer views of grass, water and sky.

It's a matter of intense personal pride for Michael to have the lawns in peak condition. 'They're part of the art of the garden,' he says, 'and what everyone's eye looks over first.' In the week before a public event, he likes to mow each lawn three times, believing that regular cutting strengthens them for foot traffic – too long and they will flatten and bruise underfoot

more easily. Always thoughtful, if he knows there'll be women in heels attending an event, he cuts the lawns a little lower so the grass is easier to walk on. His brother-in-law Wayne Bosanko helped with the lawns in the early eighties and experienced Michael's devotion firsthand. 'If any of the lawns here got burnt or damaged we would hear about it at home,' Wayne laughs.

> Well back to earth after last night's fairy tale evening – the Marquee garden & Farm looked a dream – several people commented on the Lawns – they had been lightly cut three times in six days which had a little to do with it – Dame E anxious to collect up flowers and send to friends to enjoy. ~ *JANUARY 9, 1997*

> Return a few days early from holidays to prepare for Sunday's Open Day – though garden looking a dream in this glorious spring weather the Lawns are growing at a terrific rate – edges and weeds also. Rousing welcome from Dame E. ~ *SEPTEMBER 29, 1999*

Weather brings its own timetable but Cruden's calendar imposes a schedule too. Grass must be fed exactly a fortnight before a function to be at its vivid peak. Weeds are a constant enemy but can't be sprayed too close to an event for fear the surrounding lawn won't recover in time and the Dame never liked Michael watering on the day of a function, no matter the forecast, in case it left guests walking on damp grass. She also resisted him putting in such long hours trying to keep them looking perfect.

> Dame E making a fuss about my working so late – much better to get on and have the jobs done, off my mind – rather than worry about them. Sunday Dame E in a panic that I would not have the garden ready by Friday – feels I waste too much time on Lawns & edges – but so important to the garden setting – and must be done at the right time – Picking & Walled Garden can be done Friday. ~ *JANUARY 30, 1991*

> Afternoon employed removing some of the numerous flat weeds off court lawns. Must reduce them a good deal before December 1 or the visitors I think will be rather disappointed with the quality of grass. ~ *OCTOBER 28, 1991*

On with watering of trouble spots. Worried yesterday afternoon to
see several blue grey spots appearing in Dame E's kitchen lawn
– unable to water with guests due in a few hours – just hope I am
not too late to save the grass – usually blue grey means if not
watered in few hours lawn dies off – with three functions next week
and Dame E's luncheon for 84 on Nov. 3 hope to have lawns at
their best. ~ *OCTOBER 20, 2002*

Given how much time Michael devotes to the lawns, it's understandable
that he's particularly protective of them. Well-behaved picnickers are
welcomed but careless drivers who park where they shouldn't and a brazen
lunch guest have in the past pushed him too far.

One uninhibited group set up on the front door step so that no
one could use the front door & a large group on the round lawn
which did not please me as this lawn is so difficult to keep – but
felt I could not move them in such bad weather.

~ *JANUARY 17, 1993*

Rather annoyed (to say the least) when I return from rubbish
trailer to find some woman with a death wish had opened the
second gate at Gate House entrance and drove across the lawns
– when I came upon her driving round the Weeping Elm she
quickly departed with some well-chosen words from me.

~ *NOVEMBER 7, 2002*

To minimise the damage from big crowds, the Dame limited the number
of stalls at public events, knowing that the foot traffic alongside them
would leave the 'cattle tracks' Michael finds so disheartening. Even picnic
rugs stress him, particularly the plastic-backed kind that slowly cook the
grass underneath on hot days, while on wet days crowds of visitors can turn
lawns into mud.

No real damage to lawns from yesterday's 400 plus – really does
pay to give the grass extra time and attention before these group
days – though the time I put into the lawns in the weeks leading up
to these days always concerns Dame E which in turn worries me.

~ *JANUARY 14, 1991*

OVERLEAF The seamless
flow of green, seen here
around the Laughing Tree
(*Quercus* 'Firthii') and across
the tennis court, is the
perfect stage for Cruden's
trees and flower beds.

Lawns stood up very well despite the warm day & 1200 people – even young grass in new gates area will recover – had expected to lose it completely. The feeding, watering & constant mowing every four days these last weeks really pays off – water a few trouble spots – push a note reporting no damage under laundry door – know Dame E will be concerned for the lawns & me.

~ DECEMBER 2, 1991

Michael is just as passionate about the state of the garden's gravel paths, so important in leading you around the garden, guiding the eye as much as the feet. 'Just as only some people can water well,' he says, 'only some people can rake well.'

Well raked gravel should have as much life as a good lawn.

~ APRIL 21, 1987

Morning employed raking and collecting debris from Saturday's hot windy afternoon – drives & Picking Garden paths look so different when raked – gives the garden a more loved & cared for look. *~ JANUARY 28, 2002*

His own super-sized rake is one of his most-used garden implements – with it he rakes firmly but lightly into bald patches first, then rakes so that all the gravel flows the same way. 'Just slide over the gravel to freshen it up – don't bring it all with you,' he says, showing how the hand's weight must never sit on the head of the rake. The texture of gravel, which should be neither too fresh-looking nor 'like a kitchen floor which hasn't been swept', is critical, and on paths and lawns alike, edges are treated with similarly forensic attention, kept clean but not too sharp. He still insists on raking the front circle drive himself – a chronically stiff right shoulder, just like darkness, is no impediment.

4.30am watering – rake drives through from stable – still quite dark but able to rake the drives in my sleep almost. *~ FEBRUARY 10, 2009*

5.45am – Quite dark – wind continues as I get out the ute – give my eyes time to adjust & collect barrow from compost area. Begin raking circle drive – security light at front steps coming on from time to time – though quite easy to rake in the dark. *~ MARCH 16, 2014*

In winter he looks forward to raking as an excellent way to warm up on icy mornings, and at any time of the year, he loves its meditative rhythms, for just like mowing, this is when his hands work instinctively and his thoughts can drift off, usually to plans for the garden.

> Begin raking drives and back lawns through from stables –
> had just reached side gates as Dame E called me into breakfast.
> ~ *FEBRUARY 26, 2006*

Though Dame Elisabeth worried that he laboured too hard on the lawns and paths, for Michael they have always been 'the icing on the cake' – even if achieving that perfection can be a race against the weather and the clock.

> After three careful light rakings Picking Garden paths quite
> respectable by 3pm when luncheon guests begin walking round
> garden. ~ *APRIL 27, 2001*

> Afternoon cut umbrella, tennis court and flat lawns with catcher
> mower – looking just lovely with one run to finish when sudden
> short violent wind brought down fresh new wet elm blossom
> making lawn look quite untouched by catcher mower.
> ~ *OCTOBER 6, 2001*

> Just finish running over Umbrella & court side lawns with catcher
> mower as guests begin to arrive. ~ *NOVEMBER 10, 2005*

He knows, as did the Dame, that flawless paths and lawns can always be relied on to carry the garden when flowers are scarce or the weather unfriendly.

> Light rain since 5am – had hoped to run some of the lawns over
> before the promised 4 coach loads of National Trust people arrive
> – much too damp as so often the case these last few weeks – Have
> to be happy with raking drive & Picking Garden paths. Remainder
> of day spent deadheading roses between questions from visitors.
> ~ *NOVEMBER 26, 1985*

> Afraid flowers will be in rather short supply by May 10 Open Day
> – will have to go with lawns & edges and tidy beds. ~ *APRIL 21, 2009*

OVERLEAF, LEFT
Mowing is like meditation for Michael, and a chance to think over the garden's needs and future.

OVERLEAF, RIGHT
Even if the garden is storm-battered or flowerless, says Michael, keeping paths and lawns pristine give it strength and form.

Unfortunately not everyone saw it his way, and several exasperated diary entries reveal how Michael felt obliged to defend his commitment to the lawns and paths, especially when it was suggested that mowing and raking should be left to less experienced gardeners.

> Drive just resurfaced and not looking quite the part. Mr M made the comment that raking the drives a waste of my valuable time – well meant – but not being a working gardener does not realize the importance of raking the drives and paths (icing on the cake – pride) has to my state of mind for the week's gardening. Fortunately Dame E does understand. *~ MAY 4, 1986*

> Lovely oo&r early morning walk with Dame E armed with her camera – really is the most glorious morning. Lawns looking so much better – really must not let them fall back again by listening too much to people saying Michael you shouldn't rake drives and cut lawns. Rubbish. *~ MARCH 15, 1987*

> Mr K. visiting Dame E mid-morning making the tired comment I should not be wasting my time raking – so tired of hearing this from people who do not understand the importance of the Lawns and well cared for gravel. *~ APRIL 18, 1998*

His approach to Cruden's lawns reflects too his lifelong frustration with technology and machinery – an old-school quality (he doesn't email and mostly ignores his mobile phone) that he happily nurtures. He rarely used the ride-on mower, which he dubbed 'the Red Terror' during its decade in the garden, leaving it to his brother-in-law, who loved it – though Wayne was very careful never to leave any scuff marks and always chose a far wider turning circle than he needed.

The Terror is long gone, filed away in Michael's mind with all the other peace-destroying machines he loathes so much – scrub cutters, chainsaws and leaf blowers among them. 'I bought a leaf blower last year and that was sacrilege,' laughs Wayne. Although whipper-snippers are used in the garden, Michael leaves those to his trusted assistant gardener Ken Blum, who joined Cruden in 2000 and wields them like a pair of nail clippers, while Michael's happy to keep using sheep shears for lawn edges and the small wooden-handled shovel that Dame Elisabeth was using when he first arrived at Cruden.

Cannot manage scrub cutter at all & do not intend to Learn
– noisy stressful machine. *~ MARCH 6, 1993*

My morning employed trimming drive lawn edges and back
lawns with hand shears before T. gets at them tomorrow with the
whipper snipper leaving them looking like an old chewed bone
the dog has discarded. *~ APRIL 12, 1999*

The battered state of Michael's old red push lawnmower is testament to its
years of service, and the diaries record much deliberation on the repairing
of various predecessors over the years. He and Ken now share the mowing,
taking the chance to stretch their backs after so much bending and
crouching among plants.

Afternoon Ken & I spend in company of Lawn mowers – good
balancing exercise for the old bods. *~ JULY 18, 2013*

Early in the last year of her life, the Dame suggested to Michael that she
use the takings from a large plant fair at Cruden for a ride-on to save
his legs.

I thanked her for the kind thought but went on to explain Ken
& I feel the mowers we use do a more rewarding cut – also that we
both enjoy the mowing – giving us time to stretch our back & legs
from weeding pruning etc. The Boss quite happy to leave the choice
with us – unlike those who think we are stupid. *~ MARCH 19, 2012*

As ever, they understood each other.

OPPOSITE The myriad ruffled grasses of the outer garden and farm paddocks contrast magnificently with the manicured precision of the inner garden lawns.

ABOVE A path mown through the golden fields draws the visitor ever onward.

CHAPTER NINE

Uninvited Guests

Cherry plums in cottage paddock in bloom – lovely company to the bulbs – blossom and bulbs look so well together – so country.

~ AUGUST 25, 1998

Michael's arrival at Cruden coincided with the closing of a different chapter in the farm's story, when milk from its own cows was still being churned into thick cream and golden pats of butter, just as it had been since long before the Dame and Sir Keith began bringing their young family to stay for weekends and holidays in the 1940s. There were horses, pigs, chickens and sheep then too, and the family would take eggs, milk and vegetables from the garden home to friends in town. But the old wool shed was demolished years ago, and the milking cows and other farm animals are long gone, though a rusted pig sty still stands as a reminder of those productive times.

The magnificent stone stables, commissioned by Sir Keith during the Depression to give work to local unemployed men and built using local stone, are these days used for functions and morning teas for tour groups; while the farm, once part of a patchwork of country lanes and wide fields, is now encircled by brick homes, freeways and shopping centres. But Cruden still has a pastoral heart. Hay is threshed and baled in summer, tractors rumble along its dirt lanes and a herd of four dozen Black Angus cows wander the paddocks. Kept for breeding, they're also an essential part of the garden's story, their dark velvety shapes glimpsed through its trees, flesh-and-blood symbols of that other age.

Nothing seems to deter bold crowds of swamphens from invading the garden.

It's a relief to turn off the busy road and see them ambling alongside Cruden's back drive, for while the front avenue is unforgettable, this longer dirt lane has its own pleasures, meandering as it does past the lagoon, bushy areas filled with tiny wrens and native orchids and rolling paddocks. By the time you reach the garden, the farm has drawn you into its own tranquil world. The jostling suburbs seem far away.

Such a vivid connection to its rural past is one of Cruden's great charms. But it also brings with it challenges of the kind most gardeners never have to contemplate. After all, how many suburban gardeners need worry about the devilish damage a cow hoof can do to a garden bed? Luckily for Cruden, Michael Morrison, the pragmatic son and grandson of dairy farmers, isn't easily intimidated, and with Dame Elisabeth's help, once carried a wayward calf back to the herd on her buggy.

Planted two Bric-a-Brac rhododendrons in stable bed – to replace the one stomped on by the cows on an uninvited visit to the garden last winter. ~ *AUGUST 26, 1984*

7.15am – Drove through the side gates to find the cows and their offspring making an uninvited visit to the garden – as I leaped from the ute muttering unkind words about them Dame E appeared at the side door – together we removed them fortunately with very little damage. ~ *APRIL 15, 1985*

Spent some time repairing and replacing plastic tree guards in new plantation after young calves got in last night and decided to remove guards – fortunately trees didn't appeal to their taste & only a few damaged. ~ *JUNE 11, 2011*

He's not as nonchalant about some of the garden's other visitors, especially the many tiger snakes that have passed through over the years – including one an indignant Dame Elisabeth chased from the front steps of the house, a golf club in her hand. A large specimen lived for several seasons in the old walled rose bed, vanishing into the thick catmint hedges whenever the two gardeners arrived. One afternoon when the pair were mulching the bed with pea straw, Michael worried aloud that perhaps they were inadvertently giving the snake new boltholes. 'The Boss stood up with her hands on her hips,' he recalls with a grin, 'and said firmly, "Michael, we are not allowing an uninvited guest to dictate the terms of maintenance in this garden".'

In the midst of crowded suburbia, Cruden's back drive captures the farm's utterly rural allure.

5am – on with the watering – really very dark – hope not to meet any snakes wandering about. ~ *FEBRUARY 13, 2003*

Another frequented the densely planted long border outside the back door, rattling several family members who feared it would end up in the house with Dame Elisabeth constantly banging the door so hard in her haste to get into the garden that it swung open behind her. Perhaps it was that same snake that Michael watched with horror slither out from the very spot the Dame had been weeding in soon after she went inside to make them afternoon tea one day.

Afternoon deadhead the last of the Agapanthus in Homeless plants bed while Ken attacks the blackberries which managed to get quite a hold again during summer – Ken and I think blackberries know we do not care to work in the bed during summer – too likely to run across a snake. ~ *MAY 22, 2003*

Other visitors are less unsettling but far more destructive. Bush rats manage to kill young trees by eating out their roots and feast on the walnut crop most years. Beans are carried off by field mice. Possums strip tender young gum leaves and precious magnolia and wisteria buds, despite spotlights, sprays, wire guards and Michael's fierce patrolling, while rabbits devour everything from rose shoots to delphinium seedlings. The two gardeners knew from bitter experience that every new sapling must have a tree guard when planted if it was to survive.

Rabbits determined to take House and garden over – have eaten through phone wires under drawing room. ~ *SEPTEMBER 11, 1991*

Cut cottage flat lawns again – really rather a mess with rabbits digging holes all over. ~ *JULY 28, 2012*

Magnolia denudata in full bloom the best in many years – possums have eaten Magnolia × Soulangeana and 'Nigra' instead. ~ *JULY 29, 2013*

Michael loves the resident ducks when they're at play on the lake, or dozing on its banks – but not their appetite for precious lawn roots.

Even the garden's much-loved birds can be troublesome – bright-eyed blackbirds ransacking the garden beds and excavating patches of lawn, joined sometimes by the bolder ducks on sorties from the lake. In recent years, crowds of purple swamphens have driven Michael to despair as they

sprint silently through the garden on lanky black legs to dig up grass roots and nibble lily buds.

> Ducks really quite a problem in the garden with Lake surrounds so dry – Dame E suggests we keep a sprinkler going at cottage & lake landings area in the Hope of keeping them from making such a mess of Lawns. ~ *JANUARY 2, 1998*

> Reduce the fruit trees in the hope of covering more effectively against the birds – very few pears made it inside this last season.
> ~ *JUNE 23, 2005*

Often, though, the most tenacious and irritating pests are the smallest – enemies every gardener must face sooner or later but that cause particular heartache in a large garden that has to be kept ready for thousands of visitors every year.

> Thrips waiting in the wings to come in and demolish the roses.
> ~ *NOVEMBER 13, 1985*

Michael's skirmishes over the years with pests such as thrips, aphid, snails, caterpillars and red spiders (two-spotted mite) have been epic and frustrating. An enormously heavy metal spraying knapsack, unused for some years, still sits on a shelf in the tool room, looking like it belongs more on a battlefield than in a garden. He's learnt many lessons along the way – chief of which is that when fighting off these invaders, timing is everything:

> Slipped up – missed spraying for Pear slug first week in November – slug has completely demolished standard cherry in Walled Garden. ~ *DECEMBER 9, 1984*

> 7pm – Lovely cool still evening perfect for spraying – Dame E cut wonderful collection of roses – while I prepared spraying equipment – caught sight of red spider on First Love rose foliage while deadheading yesterday – dam & blast. ~ *FEBRUARY 1, 1985*

> Cut wonderful collection of Roses & Zinnia before spraying the Picking Garden – Rhododendrons & citrus – red spider rampant

in Roses & Rhodos – Rhododendrons should have been sprayed
in November last year and were not – slack Michael slack.
~ FEBRUARY 14, 1985

If timing is crucial, weather is the wildcard that can make or break an erad-
ication campaign.

7am fine warm – some spraying with Roundup until a light breeze
came up and made it too difficult – so often happens, perfectly still
until I begin to spray. *~ NOVEMBER 11, 1989*

Roses badly need spraying – thrips have ruined all Iceberg – but
far too hot to spray – Dahlias & Shastas need spraying – earwigs
eating centres of their blooms. *~ JANUARY 4, 1995*

Weather just not been with me for spraying these last weeks.
~ JANUARY 7, 1996

Success was often a case of experimentation over many years. Different
sprays, quantities and methods were trialled and often rejected. 'There was
a spray we used a few times which would make everything look sick
afterwards,' says Michael, who these days would rather get to work on
a path with a dutch hoe than spray its weeds. 'So we stopped that.' He
remembers a former orchardist who was brought in to help – a charming
man who was, however, a little too enthusiastic, remembers Michael.
'Everyone used to get sprayed.'

Also gave Walled Garden walls a good spray with white oil – we
find this makes a large difference to how much trouble red spider
gives us in the summer – by killing off their over wintering eggs
delays their first attack. *~ AUGUST 20, 1990*

Arrive 12.20pm to find the garden alive with members of the
McClelland Gallery painting group – all very enthusiastic about
the garden especially the Picking Garden which is in dream time
– one old gent said to me you're very lucky not to have any aphids
or thrips – as I said to Dame E later – no luck about it – just good
solid hard work spraying. *~ NOVEMBER 13, 1991*

OVERLEAF Cruden's herd of
Black Angus cows are cared
for by farm manager Andrew
Gobel, whose father was
manager before him.

Also sprayed the Roses having made up my mind not to spray again this season – but could not stand the Aphids spoiling the last of the Rose blooms a minute longer. ~ *APRIL 18, 1993*

While he is realistic enough to be philosophical about the inevitability of such pests, even great gardeners can sometimes feel demoralised, as Michael was when one of the garden's few apple trees had to be cut down after being savaged by woody aphid at the same time as its fruit was being stolen by possums and bush rats.

Iceberg between weather and thrips completely ruined. Also sprayed Walled Garden – with all rain & humid weather feel sure the dahlias will be next for fungus & red spider attack. ~ *DECEMBER 10, 1985*

It was decided to remove the large *Viburnum tinus* end of Firthii bed and replace with a camellia – I will not be sorry to see this ungrateful red spider ridden plant go – endless spraying with no results. ~ *JUNE 24, 1992*

The one blot on the garden – the arrival en masse of thrips on the roses. ~ *NOVEMBER 19, 1996*

For many years, Michael and Dame Elisabeth kept up a disciplined schedule of spraying every ten days. They would roam the garden every day to check for signs of imminent attack, knowing that bugs and disease cared nothing for holidays or special events.

Christmas night sprayed roses after cutting three large buckets of blooms for the house. ~ *DECEMBER 27, 1985*

Yesterday while on a late oo&r walk with DE discovered much to our horror the first signs of Thrips in the iceberg hedge. Hence this morning's spray. ~ *NOVEMBER 16, 1986*

The spraying has slowed in recent years as pests seem to develop greater resistance, requiring more and more time-consuming and expensive spraying with no guarantee of success. 'It's like having endless antibiotics,' says Michael. 'They just stop working.' Sometimes, of course, they worked too well, as when having sprayed the Picking Garden paths for weeds one day, he drove along them too soon on the buggy and up onto the lawns. A week later he was horrified to find the grass dead where the wheels had travelled.

> More roses out each day – so far no thrips – fingers crossed – what a treat not to be using those dreadful sprays. ~ *NOVEMBER 10, 1992*

> One of the disadvantages of the mild summers seems an endless attack by pear slug on the Prunus & Pyrus – also caterpillars on the young Eucalypts – in the good old days of Nicotine Sulphate & Arsenate of Lead one spray early November took care of the problem – also I imagine any good bugs. ~ *MARCH 4, 1993*

> Aphids very thick on roses & Zinnia – have sprayed three times in past few weeks – just seems to make them stronger – next cool change will up the dosage. ~ *MARCH 10, 2001*

Though Michael jokes that all his 'good toys' – those noxious chemicals of past eras with grim names – have been replaced by harmless 'lolly water', he's glad to see the end of them. 'Though of course the tool room has no atmosphere any more without all those poisons,' he laughs. There's still some spraying done but it's kept to a minimum – if a plague of thrips mars the roses, it's quickly pruned out in the hope that the next flush of growth will be pest-free. Soil is fed more regularly to strengthen the plants and hardier varieties chosen.

> Dame E spending every spare minute in the Picking Garden removing black spot leaves – which are really quite bad for this time of year. ~ *DECEMBER 11, 1988*

> Picking garden a tapestry of colour – roses heavy in bloom – so annoying with this marvellous season – all the spoiling – feeding – composting – spraying yet still the black spot really is too much. ~ *JANUARY 19, 1992*

But even when the garden is free of bugs, marauding swamphens and disease, the weeds never let up. In summer time especially, just as the garden must look its best for the deluge of visitors, the weeds seem to grow overnight.

My day employed weeding – after her lunch guests had left Dame
E spent several hours on her knees removing flat weeds from the
Sculpture Lawn. ~ SEPTEMBER 29, 1990

My morning spent weeding through main rose beds – amazing
where the weeds come from, seems only the other day we removed
every last weed. ~ OCTOBER 4, 1994

Dame Elisabeth's great opponent was oxalis, or wood-sorrel, a highly
tenacious weed that is almost impossible to eradicate once it has a foothold.
The Boss would wage war on it over her summer break and spend hours
hunting down every stray root. 'She used to say she dreamt of oxalis after
a while,' says Michael. In later years she would come out to cheer him on
as he attacked the intruders in her stead.

Temp 40 6.30am fine clear – Dame E already well underway with
the watering – my morning employed working through the rather
neglected centre of main border – while Dame E attacked her
old enemy the oxalis in the long border among the zinnia.
~ JANUARY 7, 1988

Remainder of my morning deadheading in the Picking Garden
while Dame E made war on the oxalis. ~ JANUARY 27, 1992

Always conscious of Cruden's reputation, Michael is mortified if visitors
see the garden at anything less than what he considers to be its very best.

6.30am Start hoses – Horror of Horrors – red spider on the roses
– one rather pale looking Iceberg drew my attention – fortunately
do not think anyone noticed Sunday – so heavy in flower – spray
with Kelthane – hope I have it in time. ~ JANUARY 15, 1991

Dame E reports yesterday a screaming success – on with the
weeding in the Picking Garden – ashamed I had not weeded
among Titian roses behind Lonicera hedge – some rather unpleasant weeds – people always stop to admire the Lonicera hedge
– want to touch it & run their hand over the surface – in doing
so am sure notice the weeds I missed. ~ NOVEMBER 12, 1995

He berates himself for such oversights, and is relentlessly hard on himself if he thinks the beds aren't up to his tough standards – even if no one else notices a stray weed or two. But he reserves the right to feel a little outraged when others point them out.

One of her friends had the cheek to point out a milk thistle in the Picking Garden – I say we grow them for the chooks. *~ JANUARY 30, 1994*

Oxalis, the indomitable weed which Dame Elisabeth considered her greatest foe in the garden.

189

CHAPTER TEN

Water and Earth

The eucalyptus tang of the hot day to come is already on the air as Michael moves through the garden in the darkness before sunrise with ease, positioning sprinkler stands and smoothing out snaking lengths of hoses. He doesn't need a torch – he's done this often enough to know every shortcut and hidden tap, though it's easier if the moon is bright, when he can enjoy the inky silhouettes of trees against the sky as he begins hand-watering, their trunks casting long fingers of shadow across the hushed garden.

5am watering – garden still in dream time – wonderful soft light of full moon. ~ *MARCH 10, 2007*

Water is at the heart of every garden's fortunes and the lack or abundance of it was one of Dame Elisabeth and Michael's great preoccupations. Having begun the garden on very little water, the Boss never lost her instinct for conserving it, and expected the same of her fellow gardeners. She and Michael anxiously nursed the garden through drought and dry spells, and even in times of good rainfall their shared mood rose and fell with the rain gauge.

Dame E concerned about the Lake level with more rain forecast – is it too high? Should we drop the overflow? – But as I remind her in the dry weather she worries about the low level. ~ *NOVEMBER 8, 1992*

Dreamy early morning mist on the dam beside the stables.

OVERLEAF All of the water used on the garden is rainfall collected in Cruden's dams, the lake or in its stormwater-fed lagoon.

Dame E clapped her hands when I gave her the rain gauge reading.
~ APRIL 22, 2001

They knew that watering was one of the few jobs that could never be put off or done in a rush, no matter how late in the day or how busy they were. They understood too that knowing how often and how much to water is a skill in itself, perfected by spending decades in the same garden.

Temp 42–25 overnight – very hard on the garden & also the
gardeners – Dame E watered from early evening through until
1am when the auto sprinklers start – the large trees just sop so
much water up. ~ JANUARY 3, 1991

In Michael's first years at Cruden, the much smaller garden made do with what could be pumped up from a natural spring near the stables. In those days, when the Dame's children and their young families came to stay in the summer holidays, parts of the garden went without water to ensure there was enough for the house and its guests.

Another warm day – oh for some rain – however as Dame E and
I often think how very fortunate we are to have unlimited water
– compared to my earlier years here. ~ DECEMBER 29, 1990

A lasting image for Michael from those early years is of Dame Elisabeth dashing from the house to the pump in the front paddock to check how much water she had left. The precious supply was pumped up into the small corrugated-iron tank about 15 metres off the ground on a metal tripod beside the house, where it remains today, an empty, wisteria-covered reminder of less certain times.

It features in family folklore too, Michael telling the story of the day some forty years ago when he was shocked to see one of Dame Elisabeth's grandsons, then aged about six, scaling the narrow ladder. He was about to call him down when he saw the Boss watching quietly too. 'I went over to her and said he shouldn't be up there – she said he certainly shouldn't, but having got up there he should get himself down. She often said adults spoilt children's nerves.' Family friend and art patron the late Ken Myer climbed it too.

Mr Ken Myer while on a visit to Dame E last evening earnt his
supper by climbing the tank stand to remove a dead Wisteria

CLOCKWISE FROM TOP LEFT One of the original water sprinklers which Dame Elisabeth had custom-made; Michael at work moving heavy hoses; the Walled Garden is one of the few areas to have automatic sprinklers to help with watering.

– grateful thanks from No 2 Gardener who has no head for
heights. Wisteria died as a result of wet feet – leaking pipe –
has been an embarrassment for some time. *~ JANUARY 18, 1985*

By then, the connection of mains water had eased their constant worry and
transformed their ambitions for the garden. Two years later, the excavation
of the lake to capture run-off from the house and surrounding paddocks
would further ensure the garden's water supply. Buoyed by this success, in
the summer of 1994 the pair began discussing the need for a dam on the
other side of the stables as an additional way of capturing rainwater and
run-off.

Dame E mentioned she is considering a large holding dam put in
below stables – which has a good deal of run off – so that we would
have reserve water to top up the lake in dry years – what excitement. *~ DECEMBER 4, 1994*

With their typical resolve, just five months later that conversation resulted
in a completed dam. As with the lake, they had its clay bed covered with
topsoil – the best way, they agreed, to achieve the black water that maximises
its superb reflections.

New dam settling into the landscape more each day – by end of
spring will look as if always been – one of Dame E's best ideas yet
– wood ducks agree. *~ SEPTEMBER 5, 1995*

In dry years, the stables' dam would prove invaluable as they struggled to
keep the garden well-watered. In 2005 the small lagoon on the farm's
northern boundary was enlarged to hold local stormwater run-off, further
drought-proofing the farm, as well as adding another refuge for wildlife in
the midst of suburbia. Such foresight means that even in the harshest
summer heat, the garden at Cruden can remain an oasis of green.

5.30am – On with the watering – garden has stood up to the last two
days of high heat remarkably well owing to being so well watered up
– thank God & Dame E for the stable dam & pump. *~ DECEMBER 11, 2006*

Rain at Cruden is always precisely recorded and heartily celebrated.
Throughout his years in the garden, Michael has come in on his days off

The 'Five Ways' metal
sculpture designed by
assistant gardener Ken Blum
for the stables' dam. The
Dame would always ask
visitors what they thought
of it before adding firmly,
'We love it!'

and even during holidays to see how much has fallen. He and Dame Elisabeth would regularly call each other to relay measurements, and when the Boss is sick with a virus one January, Michael writes that he's sure the sound of summer rain on the roof 'will return her strength more quickly than anything else'.

> Rain, rain, beautiful rain. Began falling lightly about 11pm last evening and continued steadily on through the night – a light mist still falling – Dame E jubilant. ~ *MARCH 28, 1990*

> Dame E rings to welcome me home – reports only one inch of rain measured in my absence. ~ *JULY 9, 2000*

> Both like the cat with the saucer of cream as we look at the lake overflowing at last. ~ *AUGUST 23, 2001*

With such a large and beloved garden to care for, the pair's mutual obsession with water made perfect sense to them – though not always to everyone else. Walking past the house one morning after inspecting the gauge, Michael was stopped by a window flying open and Dame Elisabeth leaning out. 'How much rain was there?' she asked excitedly, before adding, 'I have a new great-grandchild!' When Michael later mentioned the conversation to one of the Dame's children, he was asked, 'And in exactly which order did she put that?'

> Lovely, lovely – light steady rain falling – began falling Thursday evening – so lovely & light – every drop soaking into the ground. ~ *MAY 3, 1997*

> Wonderful how fresh the garden looks and smells after only a few points – also makes the gardeners feel fresh & light. ~ *MARCH 9, 2004*

But when rain is scarce and temperatures soar, the watering is relentless and demanding work, with many metres of heavy hose to be dragged from one side of the garden to another, and hidden away in coils when visitors are expected. Michael would often stay until evening, or come back after dinner once guests or the sun had gone, to lay out the hoses for the morning, ensuring hot hoses couldn't burn the grass underneath and the garden still looked its best for visitors.

Roll up & remove hoses away under trees – back of court – under
Pin Oak behind stables – really quite a job – hoses long & heavy
– just as Dame E did this job herself until well into her 70s I must
not complain. ~ *FEBRUARY 24, 2007*

For many years the pair watered in tandem – when the Dame left for a day
in town, she would ask Michael to leave a list of hoses he wanted her to
turn off or move when she returned from town, often towards midnight. In
return, he would finish the watering she often began before his arrival
in the morning. In times of great heat, the trees were always their priority,
a fire cart used to drench the young trees of the outer garden and paddocks.

6.30am – glorious lovely morning – difficult to believe forecast of
30 – Dame E already well underway with watering having begun
4.30am. ~ *JANUARY 14, 1986*

Dame E helps me collect from feed room length of the old Lake
Hose – join together & pull down to pool to Maculata plantation
for Dame E to give young trees really good drink – two hours
before lunch – two after. ~ *OCTOBER 11, 1997*

Like a doctor tending to a long-time patient, Michael is attuned almost
uncannily to the garden's weak spots – he knows which areas of lawn dry
out more quickly due to tree roots or submerged rocks, which plants are
thirstiest and which areas must be watched, even in winter. He can
anticipate problems by noticing even a slight change in colour or shape of
leaf and grass, and knows the exact dosage needed to restore full health.

Lay out hoses for the morning – trouble spots have begun to show
up this afternoon. ~ *MARCH 1, 2010*

Despite the garden's size, Michael still prefers hand-watering, and
though automatic sprinklers were installed in several of the lawns and
borders some thirty years ago, he doesn't care for them – partly owing
to his aversion to anything mechanical, but also because he feels they
can hide the true state of the garden. 'They are a help but when you
water a bed yourself you keep in much better tune with what it needs
– to make sure something precious isn't being missed or something else
being flooded.'

Usual Sunday morning breakfast with Dame E – then back to the Picking Garden for me while Dame E went to church. Worried to find Walled Garden so dry in places – caught out again relying on auto sprinklers – which are not quite enough when garden in full growth. ~ *DECEMBER 20, 1987*

Dame E I think hand waters better than any gardener I know – very few have the patience. ~ *MARCH 4, 1989*

Annoyed to find the Auto sprinklers set for 1am have not been on & cannot see why – am sure these Auto things are only here to remind me how Hopeless I am with anything not manual – to make it worse the eyes are no longer what they were as I hover over sprinkler box in dark corner of big kitchen with a candle really only guessing at what I think I see. Garden a dream – thoroughly enjoy my three hours watering – very relaxing. ~ *JANUARY 1, 1999*

Although he loves being alone in the garden in the quiet of early morning, with only the birds for company and the garden waking up as he waters, Michael's dedication is never clearer than where watering is concerned.

4.45am – Came in for 5 hours' watering – which became 7 hours. ~ *JANUARY 10, 2014*

It would prove one of the few sources of tension in his relationship with Dame Elisabeth, especially in the summer of 2003. With the garden stressed by temperatures in the high thirties and damaging hot winds, Michael was working even longer days than normal and missing his days off – a tiring schedule he saw as crucial, but one that increasingly upset the Boss.

DE worrying about the hours I am working which in turn worries me that DE worried – really very difficult – the early watering not only necessary if we are to hold the garden but also a pleasure and a very calm relaxing time for me. ~ *JANUARY 23, 2003*

5am – On with the watering – continue the deadheading as morning light grows – 8am breakfast Dame E again mentions she is worried about me working too long a day – difficult – without the watering am sure we would have lost all lawn and good many

plants last Saturday – with 40 forecast for Wed before another
light cool change – also the everyday work of the garden needs to
be done – worrying really so unproductive, the summer will pass
and I'll go back to normal hours – far better to be here doing what
I can to help the garden rather than home worrying – we really
must overcome this – Remainder of my day in Picking Garden
removing over foxgloves weeding deadheading Dame E coming
out mid-afternoon to deadhead *Alchemilla mollis* along stone wall
below hedge. 8pm – forbidden to come in. *~ JANUARY 28, 2003*

In a contest of two headstrong wills, Michael eventually prevailed, and his
habits of that summer would be repeated in many subsequent years. He
confesses he didn't record many of the times he crept into the garden when
Dame Elisabeth was out or before she was up to secretly turn on a hose.
'I often wondered though if the Boss could smell the water from the house,' he
laughs. It was a good-natured battle in which the garden was always the winner.

3am – wake to the sound of rain or so I hope – have been fooled
by the wind before – but on peering out the front door yes lovely
steady rain – front terrace & garden quite wet. 4.30am deciding if
I should go to the Farm at 4.45 to water some of the outer dry
areas and be at the ready to begin raking drives at first light.
4.45am Dame E rings to say no need to come in early for watering
she has been awake most of the night and we have had wonderful
rain – she will expect me for breakfast at 7.30am. *~ APRIL 2, 2003*

5am – on with the watering – lovely to have mild summery
Christmas and Boxing Day – fortunate – making it possible to keep
promise to Dame E of not coming in either day. *~ DECEMBER 27, 2004*

4.30pm – Dame E leaves for overnight stay at Harrodine insisting
I take the morning off – however with forecast of 31 DE reluctantly agrees I come in to water from 5–8am provided I promise to
go home at 8am. March 28 – 8am home to breakfast as promised.
~ MARCH 27, 2004

The only wet days he dreaded were when Dame Elisabeth suggested that
the time might be right for his least favourite garden job. The tool room in
the stables is the snug venue for breaks with assistant gardeners, sitting on

motley chairs gathered around an old card table and surrounded by ladders, shovels, several mowers and shelves crammed with tools, coils of rope, machinery parts, gardening magazines, fly-spray, tomato sauce and plant pots. But tidying its chaos was a task Michael put off for as long as possible – even when his niece, then ten, was keen to help.

> Melanie my niece having spent last night with me decided to come out and clean up the tea area of the tool room – had a lovely time putting on clean newspaper table cloths – washing our rather dirty mugs and arranging two jars of fresh flowers – quite ready for a tea party. ~ *SEPTEMBER 22, 1991*

> DE suggests the day has come to give tool room good clean out – 12 noon tool room in shock – such a clear out – Dame E will be able to let it out for holiday accommodation. ~ *JUNE 8, 1995*

> Dame E firmly suggests this very wet morning will be perfect to make a start on the tool room – I must admit long overdue – can barely get in the door at the moment. ~ *MARCH 22, 2001*

One wet day he shocks the Boss by taking it upon himself to confront the mess.

> Later in the morning when in answer to Dame E's what are you doing – must not get too wet – I replied we were quite dry cleaning out the tool room – DE said I don't believe it. ~ *JUNE 29, 2010*

If he was avoiding the tool room, Michael could often be found not far away in that sheltered part of the garden devoted to making compost. At any time of year rakes, wheelbarrows and large piles of plant matter dominate this area at the end of the Picking Garden – pungent piles of leaves, grass clippings and soft prunings that are mulched and aged to make chocolate-coloured heaps of richly scented compost.

In years gone by, the compost would be made in several huge bins and turned regularly by the tractor. Several garden assistants with a special talent for soil alchemy have worked in the garden over the years, adding layers of soil, manure, fertiliser and some lime to the leaves to transform them into precious nourishment for the garden's sandy loam soil.

An assortment of equipment
fills the tool room, some of
it hand-made, much of it
bought by Dame Elisabeth
decades ago and still in use.

Michael loves the look of soil writhing with worms as he turns it over to the depth of his spade before nourishing it with compost. Feeding the beds, especially with the leaves of past autumns, adding to the layers of years building up in the soil, is a deeply satisfying job.

Afternoon employed covering rose beds with straw – after a second light dressing of Blood & Bone before top dressing with Mushroom Mulch – sounds rather like a layer cake – if the roses are not wonderful this year think I'll give up. *~ AUGUST 26, 1991*

My day employed barrowing compost & fowl manure to Walled Garden – finish by cutting Walled Garden grass strip – all looking very loved – 3 lovely barrow loads of 2 year old Oak mulch to cottage rock garden. *~ MAY 15, 1997*

Just as he prefers watering by hand, and will always barrow a load of compost to a garden bed rather than drive it there in a trailer, so Michael never uses gloves when working in the dirt, wanting always to feel the health of the soil. The Boss too refused to wear gloves, exclaiming delightedly, 'Just disgusting!' at the sight of her filthy hands at the end of a productive day. The notion of being connected to a piece of land means different things to different people, but there is always some of Cruden's dirt under Michael's nails.

CLOCKWISE FROM TOP LEFT Michael tending to the Walled Garden; the full rubbish trailer in the composting corner; Ken Blum and general manager John Christie weeding the new spring bed, designed by the Dame in the last year of her life.

OVERLEAF John Christie, Michael and Ken Blum share morning tea in the tool room.

CHAPTER ELEVEN

Making
a Garden

Dame E and I spent some time far side of the court – rabbiting on as
Andrew T. would say – How wonderfully the blue stone steps lead the
eye up into the strong colour of the copper beech. ~ *FEBRUARY 1, 1993*

Gardening is full of slog, unexpected setbacks and Nature's strict deadlines
– as Michael puts it, 'It's an awful job if you don't love it.' Fortunately,
for all the weeding, worrying and watering, there's plenty of reward not
just in fresh growth and flowers but in a garden's ongoing design,
in the daydreaming and planning that results in a new hedge, a changed
colour scheme or a stand of young trees. Calling for imagination, an
architectural eye and a leap of faith, it was in this difficult realm of gardening
that the partnership between Michael and Dame Elisabeth proved
especially productive.

The first structural work the Dame began alone, soon after she and Sir
Keith returned from an overseas trip in 1930 to find that planned exten-
sions to the farm's original timber homestead had gone much further than
they had expected. The newly renovated house with its proud classical
columns, extra storeys and bright white exterior seemed to the dismayed
Dame far too grand for its rural setting and she soon began planting trees
in a determined effort to diminish it.

The view of the house from beyond the lake today is a tribute to her
foresight. 'At last it's buried,' she used to say to Michael with satisfaction.
The three-storey house that once towered alone over the fields is now

The newly extended house
which horrified the young
Elisabeth Murdoch with
its grandeur.

nestled in a forest of varied leaves, from the dark scarlet of the beeches to the bright green of the elms, the tallest of which rises confidently above its stone chimneys. 'That elm stands there saying, "Well, house, you're really just a shed",' says Michael. 'The house would double in size overnight if we lost it.' The front columns that so troubled the Dame now seem modest versions of the mighty pillars of surrounding trunks.

The second event that forced her to rethink the garden's structure was the 1944 bushfire that devastated local farmland and destroyed much of the original garden as well as the orchard and silver birch grove designed by Edna Walling. Thankfully, most of the gums along the front drive recovered and though it was a terrifying event – with Dame Elisabeth and the household sheltering on the tennis court – the fire gave her a clean slate on which to begin to shape the garden to better reflect her own personality and vision.

But it was Michael's arrival with his landscaping skills, natural flair and tremendous capacity for hard work that made anything seem possible. The pair began with smaller jobs, laying the first bluestone borders with stone they salvaged from elsewhere on the farm. As their partnership developed and Michael became more attuned to the garden and its possibilities, bigger ambitions took shape – moving the roses from the original stone-walled bed, where they roasted each summer, into the open comfort of the new Picking Garden, planting hedges and more trees, shaping new beds and gradually removing old farm fences around the house to fashion new vistas and avenues.

> Late afternoon visit to cottage garden with Dame E while she explained her idea for sweeping shallow steps through alley of Malus from cottage garden to water area – really am very excited about this plan – her best yet. ~ *JULY 20, 1987*

They shared an artist's eye for the fundamental role of space in a garden and a strong instinct for the sort of structure which suited a garden of Cruden's size and character. Walking the garden with Michael now, he points out the many connections they created – between the tones of different bark and flowers, between contrasts of shade and light, and in the balance of plants arranged together in beds. With the garden as their muse, they fed off each other's insights. 'She always said I had a good eye for air and space too – we egged each other on in that respect,' Michael says. 'Though she always told the family when a new idea came up that I'd encouraged her.'

The house today, nestled among enormous trees which dwarf it, just as the Dame had intended.

OVERLEAF Looking down on Cruden gives a sense of how closely the surrounding streets and homes jostle at its edges.

Good strong strike of grass seed at citrus end of Picking Garden
– the extra three feet of grass has made a wonderful difference to the
balance of air and space – always had the feeling of being pushed into
the Picking Garden by the bulk of the citrus towering behind – the
extra three feet has given room to pause in comfort. ~ *APRIL 19, 1988*

The pair knew that good structure is as vital as it is subtle, a combination
of space, light, shade, shape and colour which must both delineate and
unify the many parts of a garden, big or small. It's not simply the curve of
a path, the height of a fence, the number of steps, the position of garden
beds, or the mix of plant colours, flowering habits, shapes and sizes through
the seasons but the playful weaving together of all these elements and more
into one harmonious picture. It determines how you experience a garden
– what you can see of it and from where, or how quickly or slowly its paths
lead you around it and to what – and when done well, the result has the feel
of magic about it.

Most exciting productive morning spent with Dame E planting
cottage steps – plant seven Malus – to give a framework to steps
and connect with apples in Long Border also the two *Malus
floribunda* either side of cottage garden seat – in time they will have
the effect of steps and planting having been done at the same time
as main garden. ~ *AUGUST 15, 1987*

Dame E so right about the urns' terracotta colour disappearing
into the paving brick colour – the eye just takes in the shape –
I was a little nervous the day we chose them – one to Dame E.
~ *APRIL 17, 1989*

The pair were always interested in the garden's possibilities, making plans
over a cup of tea or while one of them was up a ladder. On many a Sunday
morning after church Dame Elisabeth would honk the horn while roaring
up the drive to let Michael know she was home and they would be off into
the garden, 'thinking where to put this or that', as he describes it. Friends
and family remember the pair on constant trundles on the buggy, deep in
animated conversation as they tossed an idea between them. 'They would
talk about the garden and plants for hours and hours, and Michael had so
many ideas,' says the Dame's granddaughter, Penny Fowler. 'But he would
always say they were Granny's.'

Designing the gracious
bluestone steps which lead
down to the tennis court was
a source of immense delight
for the two gardeners.

215

While working in the pool area self & Dame E threw suggestions into the pot re placing of the column in the garden – Dame E suggested a dovecote or figure – mine a garden lamp – both agreed column must be in sight of side porch or front columns. ~ APRIL 11, 1985

As I sit with Dame E in the buggy under the Firthii waiting for friends we plan the replanting of side porch urns & relaying of brick path under dining room windows – with an extension to link to side porch brickwork. ~ MARCH 11, 2004

Guiding every decision was their goal of creating a large country garden settled in the surrounding landscape rather than a city garden stranded within a farm. Hence the sturdy post-and-rail fence, which curves through the paddocks, fringed by daffodils, and the gentle tapering off of benches and deciduous trees as the garden merges with the farm paddocks. Careful not to overcrowd the garden with the trees, the pair also had to be ready for the unthinkable.

Cold and damp – perfect morning for the warming job of grubbing out the four sad silver birches at pool plantation – to make room to add a Tilia to grow on for future insurance against disaster with the two large Elms on circle Lawn – so important to the structure of this part of the garden (Elm Beetle disease such a worry). ~ JULY 6, 1993

Each thought of gardening as a complete picture and were less concerned about which plants they had than how they looked together, though they preferred planting 'old friends' than the latest variety. With the structural bones of trees, paths, lawns and hedges given great emphasis, the English-style garden beds are more relaxed in design, producing a garden that is elegant without being fussy, carefully laid out but not rigid. 'There's a great difference between a structured garden and a formal garden,' says Michael. 'We have a lot of lovely structure in the garden but the garden itself is very informal.'

The pair often had their best ideas in the small hours of the morning, and would share them at breakfast, frequently finding they'd devised a similar solution. Often a plan hatched over toast would be executed by the time Michael went home, like placing a simple white bench in an alcove underneath the sprawling banksia rose covering the old woodshed.

The beautifully curved post-and-rail fence completed in 2010; one of Michael's favourite structural elements at Cruden.

Really makes a grotty hole an asset – so much for fun – on with the
deadheading. ~ *MARCH 24, 1995*

Having worked on gardens for other people who constantly wanted change
for the sake of it, he loved the fact Dame Elisabeth didn't always need
a new project to stay interested in the garden. 'There was plenty of time for
reflection and enjoying what we'd done too.'

Bigger plans, however, were mulled over for months or even years
before the Dame and her No. 2 felt they had time to properly care for a new
bed or copse of trees, or until the garden was ready for the change they had
in mind. They were content to wait, says Michael, 'because making a change
too soon, hoping the garden will grow up around it, can spoil the effect
forever'. As always, they both gardened as they lived, dismissive of quick
fixes and bred for patience. 'That's why so many people are unhappy,'
says Michael. 'If they want something, they want it yesterday.'

Early morning construct mock-up of Lake Bridge using long
bamboo canes to get side-on picture – After breakfast take Dame E
out to view my handiwork – with a few changes the answer is yes,
go ahead – so exciting. ~ *MARCH 29, 1992*

They knew too that good planning could make a structural feature as
memorable as it was useful. When farm manager Andrew Gobel built the
arched bridge in 1992 with Michael's help, the Dame and Michael first
spent hours choosing each piece of stone – salvaged years earlier from the
farm – for its markings and shape before any work began. The same
attention to detail went into blending the different ages of parts of the
garden and catering for varying ground levels in many projects, such as the
design of the wide stone steps that lead down into the Picking Garden.
Though they now look as if they have always been there, these steps posed
plenty of challenges.

They are going to be just the cat's whiskers – strong but at the
same time soft and mellow – they will date the Picking Garden
to the stables and Walled Garden period – However levels, angle
and direction will be very important to the success or failure of the
project as the steps will be marrying a cross section of levels, angles
and vistas. A good deal of eye work from all directions essential
before ever a stone is laid… Can't wait. ~ *FEBRUARY 22, 1986*

A waterfall of banksia rose
and jasmine covering the
woodshed made a perfect
spot for a simple bench.

OVERLEAF Made from
the farm's own stone, the
bridge over the lake was built
to accommodate Dame
Elisabeth's buggy and allow
two people to walk comfort-
ably side-by-side.

Their delight in tackling new projects would even apply to those occasions that threw up extra complications – when, as Dame Elisabeth used to say with her quick laugh, they found they had laid a devil's egg. In such moments, their partnership proved stronger than ever. As the Dame's long-time secretary Judy Watts puts it, 'They really were like the left hand and the right hand, working with the same goal.'

> Run light coloured rope around proposed new edge for *Quercus* 'Firthii' bed – after a little put & take with Dame E managed a line which we feel will help with the dog-eared look – being both strong and soft at the one time. Having got a line we both felt happy with Dame E then laid the next devil's egg in saying she felt worried about having too much cement and wished there was a way to extend our local stone from steps to drive – so both on with the thinking caps for rest of the morning – after lunch another conflab – the result – we will add another step & landing in stone turning the steps to come onto the lawn between paved tub area and lone brick – so simple – so right. ~ *AUGUST 22, 1989*

They were determined too to make Cruden's historic stone stables, dairy and garage central in the garden's story. Having seen many impressive examples in gardens overseas, Michael feels Australian gardeners have much to learn about using outbuildings as more than architectural footnotes. 'Australians have been great "plonkers" – if there's a vacant piece of land, we'll put a shed there.' By planting trees around them that echoed those elsewhere and complemented their stonework, they hoped to tie the buildings to the garden. 'They were beautifully built and we feel a responsibility to look after them,' says Michael, adding that they both felt it was essential to honour the farm's past whenever they could.

The clean edges and sturdy presence of the *Lonicera nitida* hedge complement the lines of the house as well as providing a wind break for the roses nearby.

OVERLEAF The stables, such an integral part of Cruden's story and structure, lit by the morning sun.

> While on an excursion to the wool shed in search of Iron supports to plant white sweet peas around – Dame E rediscovered lovely column removed from side porch during sitting room extension last spring – also beautiful old garden gate pre-44 fire – we returned to the Picking Garden with renewed determination to include these beautiful pieces in the garden. Most interesting and rewarding day shared in the garden. ~ *APRIL 9, 1985*

Nice for history of garden to have old friends do important jobs.
~ *JUNE 16, 1987*

Time out mid morn for oo&r buggy talk with Dame E taking time to drive out garden entrance to talk about position for this year's project – a form of gate house – Dame E looking at copying the side porch if we are able to match the columns. ~ *JANUARY 10, 1998*

Even when she wasn't physically involved, the Dame was never far from the action. When much-anticipated new steps to the cottage garden were being worked on one day, she was playing bridge with three friends inside – a serious weekly pursuit that Michael knew better than to interrupt. 'But the next thing I know,' he says, 'she's climbing out the drawing room window to come and have a look.' If she'd been in town while a project was underway, she'd drive around the garden in the dark on her return, inspecting progress with her headlights.

Dame E very pleased with the decision not to return the 2 fences between stables and stables' dam – wonderful for outer garden flow.
~ *APRIL 16, 2009*

As the garden expanded, they were conscious of maintaining that flow by protecting vistas from being grown over, whether that meant replacing hedges, pruning large trees or even removing them. 'A lot of gardeners can't do that because they are too fond of what's already there and they end up with a lot of clutter,' Michael says.

Morning spent in Picking Garden removing many of the rotted buds and diseased leaves from the roses – between admiring the new vistas opened up by the lowering of hedge height by 8 Ft – standing with Dame E on lower path we discovered the wonderful picture of pin oak – great tracery backed by pencil pine – far distance trees at pool plantation – much oo&ring. ~ *JUNE 1, 1986*

Though they always began with a plan, they knew that a better way would often appear once their hands were in the soil. Neither was surprised when one change led to another. 'Dame Elisabeth was so good at recreating the air and space,' says Michael, with typical modesty. 'To remain the same the garden must always change.' They were always open to new

CLOCKWISE FROM LEFT An old garden gate now used at one end of the Picking Garden was rescued by Michael and the Dame from a shed; the low entrance to the Walled Garden, with glimpses of the treasures within; the clever mix of the varying heights and colours of berberis, crepe myrtles and sedums in the Front Border.

OPPOSITE, TOP Dame Elisabeth working on a planting plan around the steps to the new lake in 1987.

OPPOSITE, BOTTOM The excavation of the original dam into the much larger lake that same year.

ABOVE The new path through the Picking Garden in late 2015, with its bluestone edging and wider outlook on the lake and paddocks beyond.

opportunities, as when two old willows had to be removed from one of the lake's small islands. The pair immediately wondered about the possibility of an artwork there, and a few months later, a striking rock sculpture was lowered into place.

> 8am crane arrives. 9am crushed rock in hole for foundation. Rock put in place – check from various points – Dame E gives the OK – most exciting – Rock sculpture looks as if it has always been – back to reality, on with the everyday jobs. ~ *OCTOBER 24, 2006*

As satisfying as such projects were, Dame Elisabeth was firm that they not be waylaid by special projects and risk neglecting everyday jobs. 'She was a great believer in keeping up with those,' says Michael. 'New projects are lots of fun but you can't lose sight of the everyday structure of life.'

> Early morning spent turning soil in Picking Garden (Zinnia & Amaranthus beds) to relieve my conscience – neglecting the garden while playing in cottage garden. ~ *MAY 7, 1985*

> Afternoon cut lawns between frequent trips to oo&r over steps – very often meeting Dame E there. ~ *MARCH 28, 1986*

One of their great triumphs (and distractions) was the decision to enlarge the old dam behind the house into a lake, bringing extra water, birdlife and exceptional reflections, but also transforming the outer garden into a park. Here, their good judgement was critical – too big and the lake could have overpowered the garden, too small and it would have seemed an afterthought. Surrounded now by trees and many thousands of flowering bulbs, with visitors often picnicking on its banks, it's very much the calm heart of Cruden, its surface mirroring the seasons and sky.

> Most exciting hour spent with Dame E & stakes – as we placed stakes for planting main bones of water area – oaks liquidambars elms willows – but not before a good deal of walking – pacing out and looking from points of garden and farm etc. – Dame E anxious to have framework of water area be a continuation of garden – and at same time marry into farm landscape – first tree planted by Dame E at 11.45am – a golden elm. ~ *JULY 7, 1987*

Thinking over what has been achieved this last year and am really delighted – and thankful for Michael's tremendous interest in and devotion to the garden and am very grateful to him for his enthusiasm and encouragement over the development of the lake. – *Dame Elisabeth*. ~ *SEPTEMBER 12, 1987*

Michael is still bringing to life the plans they had. In the autumn of 2015, work began on widening the central path through the Picking Garden to the lake and redesigning the adjoining beds – the first major project undertaken since the Dame's death. They'd first discussed the plan in the early 1990s but shelved it until the lake area had developed further, and in her final year, the Boss told Michael to begin when he was ready. Their vision, of a wider path to better celebrate the lake view and box cones in the middle of each bed for year-round structure, was realised in late 2015.

Michael is deeply conscious of the shock big changes in a much-visited garden can cause its admirers. 'But I know the Boss would be happy with this,' he says, and already the new path looks very settled, young rosemary and catmint borders softening its edges. In this way their partnership lives on, embodied in the garden.

But perhaps their greatest success together was in creating the garden's mood, such a crucial element in the making of any garden, and one which can't be planted or pruned. Dame Elisabeth always wanted Cruden to exude a welcoming warmth. Together she and Michael have achieved that, creating a garden infused with the vigour of the trees, the softness of the informally planted flower beds, the inviting vistas, and the restful lake. Filled with so many plants from friends, called just as often 'Mrs Cook's lilium' or 'Mrs Brodsky's rose' as by their botanical names, and with the story of their own friendship at its heart, the garden, says Michael, is much like the Dame herself, 'with that great strength about it but no showiness'. He could be talking about himself too. After all, the personality of a garden reflects those who love it best.

CHAPTER TWELVE

Being Away

One last walk around the garden & lake in the fading light –
to take Cruden Farm with me in my mind's eye. *~ MAY 15, 1997*

With friends and family scattered around the world, and plenty of far-flung gardening colleagues to visit, both the Dame and Michael spent time away from the garden. But their bond with Cruden was such that while they enjoyed travelling, they dreaded leaving it and even when they were far away, wandering in other stunning gardens, Cruden lingered in their thoughts.

Long walk in garden this afternoon – both loath to leave.
~ MAY 28, 1991

Dame E saying she hates the thought of not seeing Cruden for
9 days. *~ JULY 17, 2001*

Michael's first revelatory trip to Europe, in 1983, was Dame Elisabeth's idea. 'She came belting out of the house one day with a piece of paper in her hand saying, "I think you should do this",' he remembers. The brochure was for an English garden tour and the Dame was so enthusiastic that Michael booked a ticket despite knowing he probably couldn't afford it. When he told her some weeks later that he would have to cancel, she insisted she was paying, saying she had always intended to send him

With loveliness on offer in every season, the two gardeners pined for Cruden while away.

233

'for the good of Cruden'. Michael felt he couldn't let her, and politely said so. 'She said she was very sorry, she had thought we were much better friends than that – so of course I went.' The trip was such a success he was back two years later, this time under his own steam, to see French gardens as well.

> First morning back after month garden tour – didn't see anything to touch the Farm in England or France – Dame E has the garden in wonderful order – looking marvellous with the first daffs in the garden and dam bank giving lovely splashes of yellow picking up overall colour of Baileyana wattles – new violets in Picking Garden blooming well – camellias & early Rhododendrons giving soft colour in the garden – day spent with Dame E pruning 4 main Rose beds – glorious day – marvellous to be home. *~ JULY 25, 1985*

Michael has been to Europe to tour gardens a dozen times since that first trip. Whenever he was gone, Dame Elisabeth would work in the garden as often as she could between appointments and guests, making abbreviated notes in the diary in the small, sprawling handwriting of the very busy, recording its successes and frustrations and anticipating his return.

> Couldn't get home until nearly 6pm – managed some effective pottering including watering lilium and paeony bed – joy, oh joy! A beautiful pink bloom saying good evening. *~ SEPTEMBER 25, 1987*

> Am longing to see Michael – hope that he is well and has had a really good holiday – Have had a lot of appreciative visitors in his absence but do miss sharing the joys of the garden with him. *~ OCTOBER 13, 1987*

> So strange to be without Michael – the place isn't the same without him on a Sunday morning! Or on any other morning!! *~ SEPTEMBER 3, 1989*

> Did a little weeding here and there but disgusted how little I can manage! *~ OCTOBER 2, 1995*

When she was away, it seemed to Michael that Cruden was so quiet it went to sleep, and his days in the garden felt incomplete.

Wish Dame E were here to go for oo&r walk – garden a dream.
APRIL 19, 1994

7am – collect lovely bulbs flower material – arrange house flowers for Dame E's return this evening. So looking forward to breakfast together in the morning. *~ JULY 30, 2006*

With holidays avoided over the warmer months when they needed to watch over the garden more closely, trips were planned for autumn or winter, the pair having long conversations before they left about what had to be done in the other's absence and keeping in touch while away to check on the garden, rainfall and each other.

Over the morning coffee on Picking Garden steps discuss the possibility of a garden seat on the glasshouse side of the steps – to sit on and admire the Picking Garden and lake – should anyone have the time. Also spent ½ hour going through the seed basket with Dame E – deciding what should be planted in her absence. *~ JUNE 15, 1988*

So good to have the rain – Dame E went off feeling very relieved knowing we had 120 points – but saying to me as they drove out please ring Janet & let her know if we have any more rain. *~ MAY 8, 1997*

Thrilled to receive a postcard from Michael after his visit to Giverny. *– Dame Elisabeth*. *~ JULY 19, 1985*

Lovely surprise in the form of a four page letter waiting for me in the big kitchen – Dame E reporting a lovely interesting holiday.
~ AUGUST 22, 1995

They both travelled regularly to visit family overseas, with Michael visiting his sister Gay, her husband and their two children each year when they were based in Papua New Guinea in the 1980s. Flying in on a small plane over sheer-sided valleys full of astonishing flora, Michael's luggage would contain his latest photos of Cruden to share with his family in their remote village. As fascinating as he found those trips, he found it difficult to stay away, and the diaries often record his early return from a holiday. His relief in being back was heartily reciprocated, the Dame exclaiming in the diary 'Michael back, 3 cheers!' on more than one occasion.

7.30am – Lovely to be back in the garden after a month away – arrived home from PNG 2.15am this morning – four hours refreshing sleep then Home to the farm & garden to begin the tickle and polish for Dame E's lunch party … Warm welcome from Dame E first hour spent with her on a garden walk – garden a dream.

~ SEPTEMBER 23, 1989

7.30am – decided to come in first thing – rather than wait for my usual Monday time of 1pm-5pm – three weeks away could not wait another minute to see the garden. Farm looking a dream – always find the garden looks even better than in my mind's eye after being away a few weeks. Warm welcome from Dame E who rushed out from her desk to welcome me back. Roses looking full of promise.

~ SEPTEMBER 17, 1990

7.30am – Return from holidays two days early – impatient to see the garden – could not stay away another minute – added to Judy B. & Ann M. having told me Dame E's hip giving her a good deal of trouble. Very warm welcome from Dame E and Lily.

~ OCTOBER 10, 1992

In 1991 and 1997, Dame Elisabeth and Michael went overseas together to see the European gardens they both so admired, though their first trip nearly didn't happen.

Late afternoon on her way to the garages Dame E stopped off at the Picking Garden to tell me Mr Murdoch had just rung to ask for our dates in England on the garden tour – on being told we were considering cancelling until next year due to Gulf War – nonsense was the reply – get on and book. So looks like we are off again.

~ FEBRUARY 7, 1991

TOP Dame Elisabeth, pictured here at Heale House in the UK in 1991, was a lively and curious travelling companion.

BOTTOM Ever elegant, the Dame on the same 1991 tour of English gardens.

After one of their frequent 'conflabs' in the garden they decided to take her son's advice.

On those memorable trips they crisscrossed the United Kingdom by car, visiting famous and lesser-known gardens alike, often being shown around by the owners themselves. They stayed in local bed and breakfasts which they found as they drove, eating in pubs and happily bypassing grander accommodation. Arriving in Edinburgh on one trip, Dame

Elisabeth told Michael they'd been offered accommodation by a friend of hers at one of the city's luxury hotels. 'But I knew you wouldn't like that so I said no,' she reported. Instead she checked into the modest B&B Michael had booked. 'Good exercise for me!' exclaimed the Dame when she saw the four flights of stairs to their rooms. When she discovered there was no grapefruit on the breakfast menu, she bought her own supplies from the local market and took them to her table.

On each trip they covered many hundreds of kilometres, Michael at the wheel and Dame Elisabeth brandishing a map. 'She would forever be saying things like, "Michael, you do realise we're heading north and we should be heading south?" ' he recalls. Her hair always in an elegant bun, handbag over her wrist, scarf round her neck, she let him pay his own way as he wanted without any fussing and was unstoppable in her excitement about the gardens they saw, even those she'd visited before. Visiting Heale House in Wiltshire, Michael found her lying on her back in her pale-blue coat and, fearing she'd fallen on the damp path, rushed over. 'But she was just lying there to get a better photo of the weeping pear tree above,' he laughs.

She was just as keen when they arrived at Edinburgh's Botanic Gardens for a tour with the director, who asked as they set out what they'd like to see. 'Dame Elisabeth said, "All of it – but remember I'm eighty-odd, so I can't do everything." Still, every time we looked around she would have disappeared over a rockery or somewhere else.' After the pair spent time with Beth Chatto in her garden in 1997, Chatto wrote to Christopher Lloyd at Great Dixter that 'they are both so keen and knowledgeable, it is a relief, when names have dropped out of my head, to have them found for me. As you know, Elisabeth, eighty-eight years "young" now, has been over here for five weeks, looking up family and friends, visiting gardens over the country. Here, after lunch, she and Michael studied the garden in such depth, I thought we would never get round the half of it…'

They found that even when they visited them separately they liked the same gardens – they both, for instance, elected the Château de Courances, with its avenues of trees and magnificent waterways, as their favourite French garden. They came home with new seeds and thoughts of new plants or combinations of colours to try. And while not many of the sights they saw were ever replicated at Cruden, they agreed that seeing some of the world's great gardens gave them a deeper sense of what they wanted for Cruden – and of how special it was to them.

Coming home to scenes like this made Michael and the Dame cherish Cruden even more.

Have enjoyed every minute of the three weeks & all the gardens & would not have missed it for the world. Still not to be compared with those first few moments of entering the main drive of Cruden Farm – driving slowly up the wonderful drive of Citriodora to the House & garden then spending the first hour walking the garden Lake areas saying good morning to old friends – even the unpleasant grey wet morning could not take away the lovely warm feeling of being Home. ~ *JUNE 28, 1991*

Lovely oo&r buggy drive round garden & lake with Dame E – so hard to get on with the garden having DE home – the excitement of hearing about her trip – and as with me when I have been away – best of all seeing Cruden Farm with fresh eyes – Dame E cannot get enough of the wonderful winter colour of Acacias & bulbs. ~ *AUGUST 8, 1996*

Lovely long trundle – both saying garden even more lovely than we remember on return. ~ *JULY 29, 2005*

In later years, when they could leave Cruden in the care of others, they would often organise to be away at the same time so they didn't miss time in the garden together. If he arrived home first, Michael would fill the house with the garden's best for the Boss' return.

Arranged house flowers – lovely bowl of Lilac for sitting room – perfume should meet Dame E as she opens the front door. ~ *OCTOBER 26, 1992*

7am – So lovely to be back. Have been impatiently waiting since 5am for it to be time – just getting light as I get out of the ute at the stables – wait for a moment for my eyes to adjust to the early light – lovely long walk around the garden & lake – eyes taking in the shapes, forms – gradually colour & flowers as light improves – farm a dream. 8am open house and begin collecting flower material for DE's return this evening. ~ *JULY 28, 2005*

They would both return re-energised and eager to get back into the garden.

9.30am – join Dame E on oo&r trip around garden – in first 20 minutes DE arranged for Harry to move glasshouse to improve

new vista of Oaks in dam paddock from garden – great to have her
home. Very productive day in the Walled Garden with Dame E
– finished the cutting down – one side weeded and forked over
– pleasant time over the afternoon tea pot going through the seeds
and garden goodies brought home by DE – also hearing of her
visit to Cranbourne Manor. *~ JUNE 18, 1985*

So good to get my hands in the soil again – though am rather
loathe to get my unusually clean hands back into their usual state
of neglect. *~ JUNE 17, 1997*

For the last six years of the Dame's life, Michael didn't take any holidays –
as he says, 'I didn't want to miss any time with the Boss.' Instead they
reminisced about past trips, comparing old albums and memories. 'He was
so helpful to her,' says the pair's long-time friend Frankie Farrow, who first
met Michael 'as a handsome young man in his twenties' when he was
recommended by a friend to design her and her husband Ken's first garden
over fifty years ago. 'He would say, remember we did that in '07 or when we
went there – just little reminders – she had a good memory but he was like
a diary for her because they did everything together.'

While both the Dame and Michael were extraordinarily tough in the
mould of earlier generations, there were times when, despite their protests,
ill-health meant they had to leave Cruden too, as when Dame Elisabeth
went into hospital for a foot operation in 1989.

DE hated the thought of leaving the garden but all will be worth it.
~ JULY 4, 1989

As she recuperates at home, Michael brings in news of the season's first
snowdrops and camellia buds and the clean winter scent of Cruden drifts
through her upstairs bedroom window. Naturally, she is determined to be
up and out as soon as she can, surprising him in the garden one day.

Pleased to have a visit from Dame E through the dining room
window – saying she was unable to stay in bed any longer.
~ JULY 17, 1989

Very happy hour driving Dame E round garden & lake in her cart.
Much oo&ring about the trees and bulbs. *~ JULY 25, 1989*

During her occasional hospital stays in later years, the diaries record Michael visiting at least once, sometimes twice a day, on his way to and from the farm, taking in just-picked flowers, her favourite homemade lemon water and detailed updates from the garden. She missed Cruden deeply, and spoke of wishing for an open window – with the hospital just a little further along Cranbourne Road from the farm, perhaps she hoped to smell it on the air.

> Call on my way home to find Dame E in good form despite the discomfort of her leg – waiting for a report on the garden. DE very pleased to hear Ken and I have finally spent time on woodshed creepers. ~ *JULY 16, 2002*

> Phone call from Dame E to ask how I was getting on with the wet morning and would I please bring her a bottle of lemon water on my way to lunch. ~ *AUGUST 3, 2002*

As soon as possible, she was out again into the garden, enjoying – or trying to enjoy – its familiar activity and friends.

> Morning spent in the Walled Garden re-staking some of the dahlias which seem to grow before your eyes. Dame E set sail on her crutches with Mrs P. saying concentrate – no talking – no looking at the garden – this is work – concentrate. ~ *JANUARY 4, 1993*

> Dame E put in a very productive few hours removing the over material from the Alstroemeria – her longest hands on day in the garden since her hip replacement – had gone in at the end of the day feeling very pleased. ~ *NOVEMBER 10, 1993*

A lifetime of physical work has taken a toll on Michael's body too, with several injuries over the years, including many weeks spent on crutches after tearing his Achilles tendon in 2013 in a garden accident, and, years earlier, being sidelined by a cat bite that became infected and landed him in hospital, where he worried more about the garden than his own recovery.

> I feel quite useless with visitors every day at the Farm & worried Dame E will have a fall collecting material for house flowers – but as I cannot at this stage hold or lift even a teaspoon with my right

hand am rather useless. 4pm Dame E rings to say Ken will give
extra time over weekend and Joe has watered trouble spots – you're
not to worry Michael, get a good book and try and enjoy the rest.
~ *DECEMBER 7, 2005*

9am – Dr B. says I can go home – my first question can I go to
work tomorrow – yes if you're careful – you're a tough old bugger
– nice – 12 noon Home at Last. ~ *DECEMBER 12, 2005*

He's back in the garden at 7 a.m. the next day. His doctor was right, for in
more than thirty years of diary entries, there are barely a handful of sick
days recorded and it is just one short, startling entry in the winter of 2001
that contains the only mention of Michael's diagnosis with cancer, and his
need for treatment at Melbourne's Peter MacCallum Cancer Centre.

5.15pm – Dame E's guests leave giving us time for lovely long
trundle with a stop among the bulbs as I tell DE I will need time
off Sept & Oct for treatment at Peter Mac. ~ *JULY 30, 2001*

In the next entry he's back to calmly discussing plans for top dressing the
lawns. In the end, despite eight weeks of intensive radiation treatment,
Michael didn't take any time off, organising medical appointments around
his garden commitments, coming in before treatment sessions to arrange
house flowers if guests were due, and going to bed, exhausted, at 6 p.m.
most evenings.

When he told the Dame his doctor was confident he had at least ten
clear years ahead of him, her response was as pragmatic and supportive as
ever. 'We were in the buggy going around the garden and she just tapped
me on the leg and said, "Well, that will take us up to when I'm one hundred
and we'll work on our strengths after that." ' She tried to feed him whenever
she saw him during those difficult months but, says Michael, never tried to
stop him working. After all, she knew that for him, as for herself, being in
the garden was the best tonic of all.

CHAPTER THIRTEEN

Sharing the Garden

The beauty at every turn left me speechless and I slowly walked at least ten circuits of the whole area, taking in every little detail. I dallied so long I even missed my ride home! Your love of the garden is plain to see; thank you for sharing it with all of us.

A letter of thanks to Michael, 1991

Dame Elisabeth gave so much of herself over many decades of public life that no one could have been surprised if she had kept Cruden as her sanctum from the hectic world beyond. Instead, she shared the garden constantly as the setting for fundraisers, community picnics, garden tours, parties, charity events and concerts that drew huge crowds and the occasional odd request, including one from a young man who knocked at the front door one day to ask if he could run paintball sessions in the outer paddocks. 'You'll never know we're there,' he assured the amused Dame.

While they missed out on paintball, many thousands of visitors enjoyed Dame Elisabeth's generosity, with more than 15 000 passing through Cruden's gates in 2015 alone. They arrived in huge numbers – in cars, on foot, in coaches, from down the road, across the country and from around the world. In the Dame's day, some invariably appeared well before the gates were due to open and the Dame always insisted on letting them in, even if Michael was still giving the paths a final rake or she herself had just finished washing the garden benches. For many years she made sure she

Marquees were often set up around the lake to host friends, family and charity fundraisers

was at the gate to welcome guests personally, whether they were arriving for afternoon tea in the sitting room or among a crowd of thousands roaming the garden on an open day.

> Three cars coming a day early for tomorrow's Open Day – Dame E told them they were welcome to walk in the garden. *~ OCTOBER 21, 2000*

What's more, she truly loved sharing it, feeling it was the right thing to do. 'She always said, "I've had such a fortunate life and I want to share it",' says Michael. She was the guest of honour at Cruden's annual community Christmas carols performance until she was 102, and especially enjoyed seeing young families exploring the garden. She let people have their wedding photos taken there, even on her front doorstep, without charge, and if strangers rang asking to visit the garden as they couldn't make an upcoming public event, they were usually invited over. When one hundred visitors turned up mistakenly after the date of an open day was changed, the Dame and two friends showed them around the garden anyway.

Curious to her core, she was incurably interested in people, greeting everyone she met with a firm handshake and her full attention, and entertaining an incredible array of guests, from kindergarten groups to some of the world's best-known gardeners, from Dolly Parton (whose presence at a Cruden party so flustered one young waiter that he called Dame Elisabeth 'Dame Edna', much to her amusement) and prime ministers to archbishops and pensioners. While many came primarily to see her, few left without being just as impressed by Cruden.

> Dame E coming by on her way in from the garden walk to say – I can't wait to be a retired person and go off on all these lovely treats. *~ NOVEMBER 21, 1991*

> Morning spent giving drives and paths tickle and polish with leaf rake – cut round lawn – Dame E coming in from quick buggy oo&r drive said – it's all in the most wonderful order – not a thing left to do. *~ MARCH 20, 1994*

TOP A choir performs at an open day.

BOTTOM Visitors flock to Cruden public events whatever the weather.

The warmer months brought a stream of visitors, with Michael and the Boss sometimes taking several groups around the garden in a single day. They answered countless questions about the garden's history and design,

both great believers in fostering that special communion between those who delight in all growing things – what Vita Sackville-West called 'a particular form of courtesy, a gardener's courtesy'. With his private nature and quiet ways, it took Michael several years to feel comfortable showing people around the garden, though the Dame usually found him and insisted he share the limelight.

Mrs C. and friends came to see garden and lake this morning. This afternoon Mrs K. and large group of rather frightening ladies – yours truly leaped behind first convenient bush. Roses full of promising new shoots. *~ FEBRUARY 25, 1988*

Dame E showing the Calvert-Jones' English visitors the garden – they had no sooner gone than two more groups of visitors arrive. *~ JANUARY 14, 1994*

In the great gardening tradition of exchange, many visitors went home with a Cruden plant, and in return Dame Elisabeth and Michael received so many seeds, saplings and cuttings that even in such a large garden they agonised about where to fit them all. For many of these, the Homeless Plants bed, designed for 'those plants you can't place but can't be without', as Michael says, is invaluable.

Remainder of my afternoon very happily spent with Dame E at the potting bench – potting on 90 mixed plants for the Clyde Red Cross plant stall. *~ FEBRUARY 6, 1992*

Began preparing the new cyclamen bed – after much wandering & looking for the right position for Mrs T.'s generous three boxes of wood cyclamen – Dame E decided we really did not have a place in any existing beds – finally deciding to make a new bed among the birches in the cottage garden – should be ideal. *~ MAY 14, 1992*

Whether the garden was expecting two visitors or 2000, Michael has always worked tirelessly to have it looking its best, though his relentlessly high standards often leave him wishing for more time. Even when it was glowing with beauty, 'I always wanted the garden to look even better,' he admits.

The buggy loaded up with flowers for a party in the garden; Michael would ride on the back holding buckets 'while the Boss lead-footed it'.

Garden looks a dream for Dame E's luncheon – one more day's work and it would be perfect. *~APRIL 14, 1985*

Garden & lake & farm in dream time – just the cat's whiskers – Afternoon tea with Dame E by schoolroom fire. 5.30pm having promised to go home – sneak out & cut cottage lawns. *~NOVEMBER 11, 2005*

The busy calendar of events when Dame Elisabeth was alive involved much careful planning, and often meant trying to orchestrate a plant's performance weeks in advance.

Hostas wonderful do not think they have ever been better – the worry will be to get them through the heat without burn or too much colour loss at least until after the open day on January 17. *~ DECEMBER 12, 1988*

Remainder of morning employed trimming catmint edges in rose beds to hopefully bring them into full bloom again for January 9. *~ DECEMBER 6, 1998*

Cut back erigeron at base of side porch urns – hate doing it when erigeron in full bloom – lovely & fluffy but will be rather tired by 7 November if not cut now. *~ OCTOBER 18, 1999*

Despite the work and effort involved, Michael says he and Dame Elisabeth were always very conscious of not neglecting too many everyday jobs in their focus on big events.

This morning employed removing large old Grevilleas from stable bed – Dame E has been keen to remove them for some time but with so many groups to the garden has put it on hold. Hopefully yesterday is the end of large groups for a while – though Dame E has already some dates for next summer. *~MARCH 24, 1992*

With so much practice over the years the last few weeks before a big event remain a whirlwind of precisely timed activity – lawns must be fed fourteen days before an event for maximum colour and cut three times a week to strengthen them to withstand many feet. The garden is weeded, pruned, raked and weeded again. Michael has even been known to deadhead in the dark when he's running out of time, and days off are abandoned and holidays interrupted in order to have the garden at its peak. Their efforts, along with those of the other Cruden staff, have not only given so many people pleasure but have helped raise millions of dollars for charities and community groups.

> Wind drops as mass onslaught begins – day a great success – people very pleased with garden especially its condition – largely due to Dame E who has for past weeks been spending nine hour days in the beds attacking oxalis or any other weeds which dared appear.
> *~ OCTOBER 26, 1985*

> Last minute rush to cut back sad Mahonia sulking from winter move. Day a screaming success. *~ JANUARY 19, 1985*

> Dame E very keen to give me the afternoon off to make up for extra time over last week – a nice thought – but Jarrod & I really must cut all Lawns this afternoon with next Saturday's heavy traffic in mind.
> *~ FEBRUARY 7, 1998*

The day before an event is a final organised frenzy of raking, setting up tables and tents, dragging hoses out of sight, mowing and washing down benches and even the front porch columns – a job Dame Elisabeth insisted on doing herself into her nineties. Michael once found her frantically digging up phlox bushes the day before a function and, 'like thieves in the night', helped her move them in a wheelie bin to fill gaps in the Walled Garden. Finishing touches are often completed just as guests arrive, especially if the gardeners have been ambushed by bad weather.

> Be sure to lock my very untidy tool room door in case Sir Robert should be tempted to look in. *~ NOVEMBER 6, 1988*

> Sharing Dame E's breakfast tea pot while Dame E gave me a run down on the wedding – a screaming success. Continue the tickle up of paths while Dame E cleaned garden seats. *~ MARCH 24, 1996*

> Wind and steady rain last evening & early hours of this morning – yesterday's rake up of drive and paths might never have been done. Begin again. *~ NOVEMBER 18, 2001*

Traditionally the most popular time for events and tours at Cruden has been in summer when the garden is at its flowering peak – unfortunately, the very time when high temperatures and dry spells means it can be at its most stressed. Managing the demands of both visitors and the season was a difficult and sometimes draining balancing act.

Temp 37 – Lawns just holding with hoses – badly need a refreshing rain – Dame E in a panic about the friends of the Botanic Gardens visit Friday of next week – seems very worried we won't be able to get the garden in order for the visit (too much hot weather tends to sap one's enthusiasm). Must try to regain Dame E's confidence. ~ *JANUARY 4, 1990*

As I arrive Janet CJ waiting to say would I please go straight up to Dame E who has spent a sleepless night worrying about the weather & Menzies Homes garden walk today – she greets me with 'should we cancel?' – 'Certainly not' my reply – people will rug up and wear wet weather gear if keen enough. Though very wet under foot rain held off with just a comfortable number of visitors drifting through all day. ~ *OCTOBER 8, 1994*

But whether held in sunshine or mud, open days at Cruden have always been hugely popular. For many years Dame Elisabeth handed out maps and garden notes, waiting to greet long lines of people eager to meet her. In later years she joined festivities from her seat on the buggy, Michael at the wheel. One of her nurses in her last two years, Peta Kelly, remembers with emotion how thrilled people were to see her, the Dame often receiving standing ovations as the buggy made its way slowly around the garden. At other times, Michael would busy himself weeding in a central spot where he could keep a watchful eye on the garden.

11am – Visitors begin arriving – I take up position weeding in Picking Garden – good many questions of great importance – does Dame E live alone – who cooks for her – what does she eat – my usual answers, no she does not live alone – as to her diet – food – after the sight-seeing a good many keen interesting garden questions – no one asking questions had been here before with the thousands that pass through the garden – amazing. ~ *OCTOBER 3, 1999.*

With a true artist's eye for colour and composition, Michael still loves to do all the house flowers – to stunning effect.

His own ambivalence about large events at Cruden stems from one of the garden's first open days, which was swamped by enormous crowds. Police had to be called to deal with traffic jams in surrounding streets, people climbed farm fences to avoid long queues and the garden was 'pandemonium – really scary,' says Michael. 'I was told by people who saw me that I simply looked in shock.' After that ordeal it took a promise from Dame Elisabeth to use a portion of future gate takings for the garden (she usually donated them all to charity) to convince him to try again, as well as some canny logic – 'She said to me, "Well Michael, we like to visit gardens, don't we?" And she had me there.'

> Tuesday over and so on to the next event – next Wednesday's Children's Hospital auxiliary – 200 for a garden lunch – just a nice number. ~ JANUARY 21, 1989

> Despite the dreadful weather still 700 visitors to the garden – all I spoke to had not been here before – Am grateful for the bad weather – am sure if it had been fine & sunny we would have had a stampede like five years ago. ~ NOVEMBER 6, 1994

Once the crowds have gone and the front gates are closed, the stocktake of the garden begins, with the state of the lawns always Michael's first concern.

> Fine clear morning – rake front drive and Picking Garden paths (to put some life back into gravel after yesterday's pounding). Garden came through yesterday's stampede very well – nice to see so many people enjoy the garden. New grass under drawing room and sitting room windows flattened with people trying to look inside. ~ OCTOBER 27, 1985

> 4.40am – water worst of trouble spots – at breakfast DE says never again – no more commercial stalls other than food or drink – garden & House covered in dust. ~ OCTOBER 22, 2007

Although the Dame's house was off-limits during such events, that didn't deter the stickybeaks, people frequently climbing through garden beds to peer inside, and several even found wandering around upstairs. Dame Elisabeth would simply wave if she was at home when people gathered at the window but Michael was always incensed, as he was when he felt her generosity was taken for granted.

People really do take Liberties – Dame E made it quite clear on day one no PA – spoils the tranquillity of the garden. ~ *FEBRUARY 13, 1998*

Garden & lawns held up very well – other than the five bags of rubbish left in the garages where tea & coffee were being sold – amazing to leave their rubbish for Dame E to deal with – so many groups do – as if they were paying a large fee to use the Farm – really wish we could have a check list of dos and don'ts to give these groups. ~ *OCTOBER 4, 1999*

Therese discovered three rather pushy Ladies swimming in the pool – no bathers. ~ *FEBRUARY 15, 2007*

He writes in the diary of his fury too when a TV garden show rings Dame Elisabeth asking to change the date for its filming visit for the third time.

Dame E much too soft – three times and you're out would be my reply – instead Dame E has been worrying during the night how she can fit them into an already very busy day on the date they have asked for – also worried in 3 weeks the garden will be over. ~ *MARCH 20, 1997*

Away from the crowds, media requests, parties and black-tie fundraisers, family events such as weddings, with dance floors set up on the tennis court and marquees beside the lake, gave the pair the chance to have enormous fun arranging table decorations from the garden – and giving them all away at the end of the night.

8.30am – breakfast with Dame E then load up buggy with beech & wonderful 4 Ft tall oriental Lilies – while I sit on the back & balance two buckets Dame E carefully drives us to tent – wind a problem. 3.30pm Wind has dropped a little but still gusty – Dame E & I arrange four urns of white Oriental lilies – mock orange & Green Goddess – also a few arching canes of Edna Walling roses in bloom – carefully picked from woodshed climber so as not to be missed. ~ *NOVEMBER 30, 2002*

Their workroom was the light-filled kitchen, nicknamed Clapham Junction by one of Dame Elisabeth's friends for its bustling atmosphere before a

big event. With its floral wallpaper and old melamine table, its many shelves cluttered with vases and a basket of lemons on the window sill, it's the very picture of a homely country kitchen. Here is where flowers cut from the garden (or donated by gardening friends to keep Cruden's beds intact) were amassed, prepared and skilfully arranged in large urns or dozens of table bowls by Michael, the Boss and friends and family who teamed up to help them.

> 6am – Make a start on flowers – first the lovely silver goblet for big sitting room – using lovely lilac – first of season – rhododendrons azalea & Doris Downs rose – rather larger arrangements than usual but with 80 people in the house tomorrow think we can go a little over the top. *– OCTOBER 25, 2003*

Michael still makes beautiful bouquets here, for old friends of Cruden, his colleagues and the Dame's family. He can still pick out any vase and recall which event it was used for and what it was filled with, such as the 250 water lilies painstakingly picked and then transported in buckets from a friend's dam to decorate the marquee when the Dame turned eighty in 1989. Here too, they worked as a team – Dame Elisabeth writing all the invitations and place cards and deliberating over seating arrangements on an easel set up in her bedroom, while Michael put in even longer hours than normal to ready the garden, the pair then coming together to decorate the tables with the garden's finest flowers.

Despite her children's best efforts in later years to ensure she left the more strenuous work to others, the Dame couldn't be convinced to delegate, typified in the run-up to her seventieth birthday party when she was found, despite an injured shoulder and having agreed with her daughters that she would rest, up an extension ladder fixing a flower arrangement that was perched on top of a tent pole, a very nervous catering company employee holding the ladder steady.

> 6.30am – Big kitchen looks like a florist full of lovely bowls of flowers – Dame E must have worked late into last evening – rather the pot calling the kettle black telling me to stop last evening – rather annoying – DE nervous about tonight and decided to be on the safe side and have a tent – However by mid-afternoon lovely warm sun – will be a perfect evening. My morning employed giving Picking Garden a tickle & polish – afternoon rake drives & give

Michael at work in the big kitchen, the site of countless preparations with the Dame for special events at Cruden, now full of memories and vases.

> Walled Garden a final tickle – as always the odd area would love to have spent time on but guests arriving 5.30. ~ *FEBRUARY 1, 1991*

When Michael was fifty-nine, the Dame told him while she wasn't ready for him to turn sixty, she'd decided he had to have a party. 'I said, "Thank you, but I'm not really a party person",' recounts Michael. 'She said, "Nonsense, we must celebrate – and anyway some of your friends have already accepted".' He remembers a wonderful lunch held in his honour at the house for twenty-nine friends and members of both his and the Murdoch families.

> Lovely trundle with Dame E returning to afternoon tea by the schoolroom fire & guest list for my 60th birthday luncheon & addresses for DE to write – I suggest she put no presents please on invitation – Dame E very strongly against the idea. ~ *JULY 6, 2004*

Determined to keep Cruden at the heart of her family's life, Dame Elisabeth also wanted to share what she was convinced was the soul-nourishing effect of being surrounded by beauty. With Michael's help, she achieved both. One of his favourite memories of sharing Cruden is of Dame Elisabeth relishing the chatter and festivities around her, shoes kicked off and her feet resting contentedly on her beloved Lily who lay, close by as always, under the table.

> Lovely crowd – really quite a picture with people picnicking around the tennis court & walking in the garden – think Dame E enjoyed it more than anyone. ~ *NOVEMBER 30, 1997*

The Dame and Lily at Cruden in a rare moment of rest.

CHAPTER FOURTEEN

A Life in the Garden

The Dame's great love of her garden and life did not dim with age. At 102, she was deciding where to plant new trees, inspecting new fences and ordering roses with Michael. At 103, the pair were designing a new spring bed and she was still playing bridge, with Michael making a posy for her playing partners, as he had for decades. The pair would lunch together at nearby McClelland Gallery and Sculpture Park, of which she'd been a major supporter, having affogato at their regular table, or drive to one of her daughters' homes, talking all the way there and back about the garden. Sometimes he would take her to one of their favourite nurseries high in the hills, where she would wait in the car while he walked its steep terraces and came back to tell her what looked best. On their return they would drive around the farm, savouring the work of a lifetime but always with an eye to the future.

The Boss had suggested a double drift of bluebells around pear tree below Gate House & also under Oak. ~ *JUNE 25, 2012*

Lovely long drive round farm & outer garden – the Boss thrilled with the early drifts of bulbs. ~ *JULY 15, 2012*

Even when she wasn't strong enough to go out into the garden, the Dame still longed to see it, spending one winter's afternoon watching old episodes of garden shows featuring Cruden. And in the final few months, when she

Ken Blum's bust of the Dame amongst honeysuckle blossom in the Walled Garden.

spent her days resting in the schoolroom, Michael brought the garden to her. Every morning he filled the room with armfuls of whatever was in flower, and shared the garden's news, telling her of jobs done and jobs to do, describing scents and new shoots as vividly as if she were walking among the beds herself. 'She never lost her interest in the garden,' he says now, 'even if she was asking with her eyes closed what was in flower.'

Dame E in good form after good night's sleep & as always very appreciative of the flowers – naming each as I take them into schoolroom. ~ JUNE 10, 2012

The Boss keen to know what is in bloom – looking forward to coming into the garden soon. ~ OCTOBER 15, 2012

More roses out each day – take in collection for the Boss before leaving – Dame E asking if any Lily of the Valley out in the garden. ~ OCTOBER 22, 2012

On one of her last visits to the garden the Dame sat contentedly looking at the Picking Garden in its spring joyfulness, and when she died peacefully at home on December 5, 2012, at the age of 103, the elms she had planted eighty years before were in bright leaf just outside her window. Three days after her death, Michael returned to the diary.

Garden in dream time. Dame Elisabeth Murdoch roses in full bloom. ~ DECEMBER 8, 2012

At both the Dame's state service in Melbourne's St Paul's Cathedral, for which he arranged her beloved copper beech and elm foliage with roses and gladioli, and at the private gathering held by the lake at Cruden, Michael sat with her family. He took comfort from knowing how much the garden was in her thoughts until the day she died. 'I would have found it very hard to bear if she had spent those last two years when she was frail waiting to die but she was so involved and interested right up to the end,' he says. 'I just think how very fortunate I was to spend such a long time with her.'

The ivy-clad doorway from the Walled Garden with the shimmering elms beyond.

5am – with 37 hot north winds forecast – start hoses early – 5.30am quick dip in the pool before the next hose move – my lower back is

complaining about moving the sprinklers & long hoses – I know the
Boss would say some exercise in the pool will help. ~ *JANUARY 24, 2013*

The Boss very much with me today in thoughts. ~ *DECEMBER 5, 2015*

He most misses hearing her voice, her lilting way of calling 'Mi-chael'
across the garden, wanting to ask his advice or share a clever idea. But in
his memories of her, he feels she is still everywhere at Cruden – happily
scrubbing gladioli bulbs on a sheet of newspaper in the front hallway on
a wet afternoon, clapping her hands with glee after a downpour, roaring
along on the buggy among the huge oaks they'd planted, or finding him in
the garden with their morning tea. The years have sped by so fast –
'in a flash', as he says – and it seems not long ago that his young sister came
to find him in the garden to show him her engagement ring, though she
has now been married for more than forty years.

Decide perfect opportunity to redo the white Belladonnas along
the plantation side of pool wall – Dame E suggested their poor
flowers in past two years may be from being too crowded – my
first thought was not all that long since the bed done – DE smiled
and said Michael, your 'not too long' is 28 years – the bed last
done when roses moved and pool put in. ~ *APRIL 13, 2009*

Lovely peaceful morning in the garden – rather reminds me
of early days when the Boss would go to church – come home
& give me morning tea on the side porch. ~ *JANUARY 13, 2013*

There's barely a plant that doesn't remind Michael of their time together.
Here is the lemon balm that she always picked a sprig of for its sharp scent;
there the magnificent rhododendron whose mauve flowers decorated the
tables at a lunch to celebrate Michael's forty years at Cruden in 2011,
chosen by the Dame because it was one of the few remaining plants that
predated her own arrival as a young bride in 1928.

On a spring day full of such vitality you can almost see the garden
growing, Michael stops beside the stables to admire the white flowers of
the climbing hydrangea, *Hydrangea petiolaris*. He first saw these plants in
English gardens more than thirty years ago, and returned to Cruden
singing their praises. They were hard to buy in those days but a few weeks
after he arrived home, the Boss gave him a young potted specimen.

The Dame with her dog Sally
at the same doorway, so at
ease in her beloved sanctuary.

267

She'd tried growing them several times before his time, she explained, without success. 'But I thought I would try one more, for you,' she said. That vine now covers much of the honey-coloured stone wall.

Cruden is today overseen by a board of trustees comprised of Murdoch family members, but Michael still feels he is working for the Boss, asking himself whether she would approve of every decision and new plant. As fellow gardener and friend Ken Blum puts it, the Dame's vision for Cruden lives on very strongly through her No. 2: 'He knows what she had planned – he says, "she would love this" or "she'd be sorry about that".' Soon after her death, Michael planted snowdrops under the hawthorn as she'd wanted, and took out the old cedar as she planned. Describing the healthy growth of the plantation of spotted gums, *Corymbia maculata*, in front of the stables, he remarks, oblivious to his tense, 'She's hoping you will look eventually out on those trees and through to the paddocks.'

Gardens like Cruden are works of art but, unlike sculptures or paintings, they are ever-changing masterpieces that are never truly finished, nor protected in museums or behind glass. Their artistry is more fragile and their greatness can be erased by weeds, neglect or suburbia. Michael has seen other gardens suffer that fate, and is thankful that the Dame's family has a deep respect for its history and a commitment to its future. 'We all feel that she is watching over us there. We all want to make sure the garden is an ongoing thing for Mum's sake – that is what she wanted,' says Janet Calvert-Jones.

> Very important for her family to get to know Dame E the gardener
> – How and why she plans – How she feels about the garden & Farm
> – if the garden & Farm are to go on – important that family members
> understand and have a feeling for its wellbeing. ~ DECEMBER 31, 1990

Nevertheless, the Dame always wanted Cruden to one day be able to support itself financially, says Michael. 'She'd find it depressing if it didn't stand on its own two feet,' he says. Her great wish was that it remain a community asset, its enriching beauty to be enjoyed by as many people as possible. But, as she often confided to Michael, she worried about the responsibility she was leaving her family. 'She would say you just have to travel in hope,' he recalls.

Historic gardens elsewhere, such as Great Dixter and Sissinghurst, have thrived because while preserving the mood and intent of their original design, they have kept evolving, and there is much discussion about how Cruden might do the same. Of his own future, Michael has never considered retiring, though he knows his body is slowing and can no longer do as much as it once could. In the meantime, he keeps looking after the garden for, of course, it waits for no one.

> 6.30am Lovely mild still spring morning – Watsonias at front gates amongst the wonderful lemon-scented trunks still in full bloom – so lovely in the early morning light – really their best flowering for some time I think – though the Boss would say that about most plants each year. ~ *NOVEMBER 16, 2013*

> I go on with clean-up of diseased Rose leaves from main beds in Picking Garden – the Boss has always been very firm on the importance of picking up as much of the black spot leaves as possible before spraying feeding & forking over beds. ~ *JULY 15, 2013*

The house still feels as though the Dame might arrive home any moment, with the fires set, Michael placing flowers where she always liked them, and a pile of her books beside her armchair in the schoolroom. He begins work in the dark, examines new blooms with genuine delight, and takes visitors around on the Dame's buggy, though perhaps at a less hair-raising pace than she would have liked. Community days and charity events continue to attract thousands, and Bonnie waits on the back porch, impatient as ever, for her daily run around the lake.

She barks a welcome when Michael arrives each morning to walk the front drive, passing as he does a young lemon-scented gum, dwarfed for now by its neighbours. It was planted in memory of the Dame in the year after her death, and it seems certain the Boss would have approved of the fact that her tree is not showy or feted, but an integral part of a larger story. Michael has his own tree too, a young dark-leafed tri-colour beech by the lake, which he planted, watched by the Dame and their two families, in the spring of 2011 to mark his forty years at Cruden. He likes the thought that, in time, it too will become part of a tapestry of foliage, and that these trees will live on long after those who planted them have gone.

> Weather on the warm up – garden a dream – say this so often – but then to me the garden is always in dream time. ~ *NOVEMBER 20, 1990*

When Michael walks Cruden now, he travels in his mind's eye through several landscapes at once: the garden that was, full of those people and plants that have grown and gone but are still remembered, the garden as it is now, tranquil and welcoming, and the vibrant garden he hopes it will be when he is no longer there. He lives by the Dame's ethos, which gave her such strength: gain comfort from the past, live for the moment and look forward to the future. And when her namesake roses begin blooming each spring, in that season of great energy and optimism, he puts a single rose in a vase on her table.

OVERLEAF Michael walking Bonnie around the lake, surrounded by his life's work.

Acknowledgements

Michael would like to thank the current staff of Cruden:

Ken Blum, gardener
Dale Cowan, gardener
Amanda Woodhams, gardener
John Christie, general manager
Andrew Gobel, farm manager
Peta Kelly, housekeeper
Barbara Schuyler, administration

Michael would also like to thank those who helped him at different times in the garden over the years, including:

Tony Gobel
Harry Gobel
Joe Wilkinson
Camilla Graves
Darron Ogiers
Craig Ogiers

Glenn Ogiers
Andrew Tabner
Jack Goudie
Hubert Sonnefeld
George Capuano
Sam Christie

Les Johnson
Ron Nobelius
Jarrod Bosanko
Wayne Bosanko

From Lisa Clausen:

My thanks first of all to John van Tiggelen, who was editor of *The Monthly Magazine* when I suggested writing about Michael in 2013, and who published the article which led to this book. Many thanks also to Julie Gibbs of Lantern Books, who pursued the idea, and to Katrina O'Brien of Penguin Random House Australia, for her wise counsel along the way. Between them, photographer Simon Griffiths and designer Daniel New have captured Cruden magnificently. I'm very grateful to Penny Fowler for her support and memories of her beloved Granny, and to Peta, Barb, Ken and John at Cruden, who shared stories, photographs and cups of tea with me. It's been a privilege to spend so much time in the garden with Michael, whose private nature must have been tested at times by my endless questions. He answered each one with patience and good humour, and his story has been a delight to tell. Above all, to my family – with love and gratitude comes my wish that you will always know the joy of words and stories, and of planting and sharing gardens of your own.

Index

LANTERN

UK | USA | Canada | Ireland
Australia | India | New Zealand
South Africa | China

Penguin Books is part of the Penguin Random House group of
companies whose addresses can be found at global.penguinrandomhouse.com.

First published by Penguin Random House Australia Pty Ltd, 2017

Design and map by Daniel New © Penguin Random House Australia Pty Ltd
Typeset in Janson Text
Garden photography by Simon Griffiths except for p.272 by John Christie
Historical photographs pages i, 7, 8, 14, 25, 31, 36, 208, 228, 237, 250, 261, 266, 270 reproduced with
the permission of the Murdoch family
Historical photographs page 13 reproduced with the permission of the Morrison family

Colour separation by Splitting Image Colour Studio, Clayton, Victoria
Printed and bound in China by RR Donnelley Asia Printing Solutions Limited

National Library of Australia
Cataloguing-in-Publication data:

Creator: Morrison, Michael, 1944- author.
Title: Cruden Farm Garden Diaries / Michael Morrison ; Lisa
Clausen ; Simon Griffiths.

ISBN: 9781921384158 (hardback)

Notes: Includes index.
Subjects: Cruden Farm (Langwarrin, Vic.)--History.
Historic gardens--Australia--Langwarrin (Vic.)
Gardeners--Australia--Langwarrin (Vic.)

Other Creators/Contributors:
Clausen, Lisa, author.
Griffiths, Simon (Simon John) photographer.

Dewey Number: 712.609945

penguin.com.au